Lament as Discipleship
Walking and Crying out to God with One Another

Patrick Testerman

Flying T Press, Chichester, New Hampshire

Lament as Discipleship: Walking and Crying out to God Together
Copyright ©2024 by Patrick Testerman

ISBN: 9798883990563

All rights reserved. No part of this publication may be reproduced, stored in a retrieval system, or transmitted in any form by any means, electronic, mechanical, photocopy, recording, or otherwise, without the prior permission of the author, except as provided by USA copyright law.

Scripture quotations, unless otherwise indicated, are from the ESV® Bible (The Holy Bible, English Standard Version®), copyright © 2001 by Crossway, a publishing ministry of Good News Publishers. Used by permission. All rights reserved.

Scripture quotations annotated (NASB) are taken from the (NASB®) New American Standard Bible®, Copyright © 1960, 1971, 1977, 1995, 2020 by The Lockman Foundation. Used by permission. All rights reserved. lockman.org.

Names: Patrick Testerman, author

Printed in the United States of America

DEDICATION

In His "High Priestly Prayer" in the 17th chapter of John's Gospel, Jesus prays not only for His disciples, but for those who would believe in Him through those disciples. It was humbling and frankly mind-blowing when I realized that Jesus was praying for me. It is even more awe-inspiring to me to try to imagine how, over the next two thousand years, Jesus' gospel made its way into my heart. I don't know all the disciples of Jesus through whom this gospel passed, but I must name some of them.

First, my parents, who discipled an often-rebellious child by giving him a foundation of faith that he did so much work to distort and run from.

Jim Slagel and Clem Boyd took that rebel under their wings and patiently pointed to the real Jesus until I finally saw Him.

Father Mike Williams was not the first to practice the ministry of presence in my life, but God used him to illustrate it powerfully.

Dr. Jim Bruckner taught me of God's gift of lament, a practice I now consider a spiritual "comfort food."

Jack Hill discipled me in the ways of Jesus in a manner that made discipleship become a way of life.

God brought Nick Clark into my life for many reasons, but I think one of the most important was for me to learn kindness, and that God Himself is kind.

The people who are Faith Community Bible Church have loved me beyond measure, including through the gift of regular sabbath and the sabbatical, during which I wrote most of this book.

Several friends walked with me during the editing process, but Dave Grigoryan stands out among them for his exhaustive and patient work

God has used so many others in my journeys of discipleship, suffering, and lament, and you will meet some of them in this book.

The person He has used most powerfully has been Martha, the woman He brought alongside me as my wife. For over thirty years, Martha has faithfully loved me, comforted me, honored me, kept me, loved me, and cherished me. She has done this in times of great plenty and great want, in well-being and calamity. She has discipled me and discipled our three wonderful children, now adults. She has discipled me in our suffering, and her witness in suffering has grown my faith in Christ and my love for her. She has lamented alongside me. Of the myriad ways God has shown his *hesed,* what the KJV translates as "lovingkindness," to me, Martha stands out.

God is kind.

Soli Deo Gloria.

Table of Contents

Dedication 1
Introduction 4
Part 1: Setting the Stage 16
   Discipleship... 16
   Suffering 26
   Biblical Lament 39
Part 2: Discipling into Suffering.. 54
   Called Alongside 54
   Showing up: The Ministry of Presence 58
   Inclining Our Ears: The Ministry of Listening 74
   Sharing in Suffering: The Ministry of Empathy.......... 87
   Crying out Together: The Ministry of Lament 94
   Discerning and Responding: The Ministry of Counsel 103
   Staying close: The Ministry of Persistence 118
Part 3: Discipleship from Suffering 125
   Suffering from the Front 125
   Growing: Conforming to Christlikeness in our Suffering.... 128
   Inviting: Allowing Others into Our Suffering............ 134
   Opening: Vulnerability and Transparency 145
   Modeling: Suffering as Witness to the Gospel of Christ 163
   Teaching: Passing on What We Have Learned 172
Conclusion 177
Appendix 179
   Suggested Scriptures 179
Bibliography.. 182
About the Author 187

INTRODUCTION

A Journey of Discipleship, Suffering, and Lament

All humans suffer. While some religions and philosophies seek to deny, minimize, ignore, or otherwise separate suffering from our existence, Christians believe in and follow the God who *chose* to join us in this suffering and called us to become His disciples and follow Him. Instead of offering an easier path in which people could set our suffering aside and fulfill our desires, He called those who would follow Him in this journey of discipleship to deny themselves and take up their crosses. And rather than demanding sufferers to remain stoic or silent, Jesus calls us to join Him in lament, crying out to the only One who knows, sees, comforts, responds, and is sovereign in our suffering.

This is the journey to which Jesus calls sufferers, a journey He calls us to walk with Him and with others He brings alongside. I hope this book will assist those who seek to walk this journey by helping them understand and embrace the relationship between suffering, discipleship, and lament.

My Journey

I began this writing project at the start of my first pastoral sabbatical, seven years after entering vocational Christian ministry, which I did somewhat late in life. I used the term "vocational" intentionally. While some are called to paid Christian ministry, every aspect of every Christian's life is the ministry to which we have been called. God calls some Christians to lead, equip, and build up His Church as their full-time occupation, but every Christian is set apart for the work of Gospel ministry.[1] At Faith Community Bible Church, we see this ministry fulfilled in the Gospel mission to glorify

---

[1] Eph 4:11-12.

God by multiplying disciples, leaders, and churches through four mission areas:[2]

- Proclaiming the Gospel,[3]
- Making Disciple-Making Disciples,[4]
- Supporting Missionaries,[5] and
- Equipping the Church[6]

Within those areas, the call to discipleship has a special place in my heart. Our journeys are intertwined with the paths of those who are mature (or more mature) in Christ. Their paths intersect with our own to help show us the Way. As we mature in Christ, our journeys will likewise bring us alongside fellow travelers whom we have been called to help. This is discipleship in its most basic form – one person walking alongside another, helping him or her grow in Christlikeness. As I have walked and been walked with in this sacred practice, discipleship has:

- Changed the way I understand and experience suffering,
- Helped me see God's blessings and purposes through being discipled *in* my suffering and discipling others *from* my suffering, and
- Introduced me to God's gift of Biblical lament for sufferers called to discipleship with other sufferers.

My Journey of Discipleship

Being discipled and making disciples has completely changed my experience and understanding of suffering.

Discipleship means different things to different people. For the purposes of this book, I will define it as "pouring our lives into intentional, Christ-centered, Scripture-based, prayer-covered, love-

---

[2] Faith Community Bible Church, "Elder Vision Priorities," (Loudon, New Hampshire, 2018).
[3] Ps 96:3; Acts 1:6; 13:47.
[4] Mt 28:18-20; 2 Ti 2:2.
[5] 3 Jn 5-8.
[6] Acts 4:32-37; 6:1-7; Eph 4:11-16; 2 Ti 3:16-17.

soaked relationships with others, helping them know Christ, teaching them obedience to what He has commanded, and growing together in Christlikeness." And one of the things that Christ commanded was for us to teach others to do likewise.

I came to faith in Jesus Christ through discipleship. I cannot discount the work that was done in my early life, growing up in a church-going home with loving and caring and involved parents. However, two disciple-makers, Jim Slagel and Clem Boyd, helped me over the hurdle of coming to saving faith in Jesus through their focused and intentional work. Jim was my high school physics teacher, and Clem was a missionary with Youth for Christ. Together, they led the local chapter of a ministry called Campus Life.

I enjoyed some of the get-togethers that Jim and Clem held, but I believe God used the personal encounters with them to change my life. Through discussions after lunch with fellow students and Jim and his wife at their house, or over a root-beer float at the A&W with Clem, I began to learn about Jesus as a person rather than a storybook character.

I continued to go to church with my family on Sunday mornings but started attending a home church on Sunday evenings with Clem. There, we dove more deeply into the Bible and prayer, and I began to understand the essentials of the Gospel. For the first time I understood that like everyone else since Adam and Eve, I had sinned against God Himself, that those sins had earned me death, and that only through Jesus could I be saved from those consequences. It took some time for my heart to embrace what my head understood, but I thought I played a pretty convincing game of being a Christian. My heart finally broke one night, and I confessed this ruse to the members of the home church, asked Jesus for forgiveness, and began my life in Christ.

Decades later, I reconnected with both Jim and Clem. Clem told me that I did not fool anyone.

My adolescence ended and I headed off to college, and then into marriage and the military. Throughout the subsequent decades, pastors, ministry leaders, Christian friends, and my wife poured into my life and faith. When my career required getting an advanced degree, I spent my efforts, resources, and leave at our denomination's seminary which had just begun a hybrid program with online and in-person intensive classes. Though my degree concentration was in Evangelism and Discipleship, and while both my wife and I were committed servants in our churches, leading Bible studies, Sunday school classes, small groups, and other ministries, I continued to dabble rather than commit to true discipleship. It wasn't until two years later that the light bulb came on.

Twenty years after I became a Christian, my wife and I moved from overseas back to the states and I was on track to take my first squadron command. As these years would be challenging in multiple ways, I knew I needed someone to help lead me through those tests if I was going to survive with my faith, family, and integrity intact. I called the local Navigators missionary Jack Hill, and asked if he would disciple me.

Jack invited me out to lunch and asked what I meant by discipleship. I had many ideas; someone to hold me accountable, to listen to my struggles, give me wise counsel, and to pray for me. While I knew all of those were aspects of discipleship, and *even though* I had a seminary degree with a concentration in "Evangelism and Discipleship," I really did not have a concrete definition of what "discipleship" was.

Jack did. Over the next years, he taught me what discipleship was by showing it to me. We met almost every week, starting with Gospel basics through the study, *Lessons on Assurance*,[7] then continuing into book studies and the *Topical Memory System*,[8] all classic Navigators fare. True to Navigator form, Jack pushed me to start discipling others. When I resisted, Jack kept pushing.

---

[7] The Navigators, *Lessons on Assurance: Five Life-Changing Bible Studies and Memory Verses for New Christians*, (Colorado Springs, CO: Navpress, 2007).

[8] The Navigators, *Topical Memory System* (Colorado Springs, CO: NavPress, 2020).

It was then, when I started discipling others the way that Jack had discipled me, the light bulb finally turned on. I have tried to explain to people what that experience was like, and here is what I think is a best attempt, based on two of my passions – flying and fly fishing.

I can talk to you all day about either of these pursuits. I can explain aerodynamics and stick-and-rudder concepts, or fish biology and casting techniques. I can extoll the experience of throwing a jet's motors into afterburner and pulling "Gs" around a towering cumulus cloud, or the way my heart nearly explodes waiting for just the right moment to set the hook as a salmon is racing at my dry fly, throwing a wake like an inbound torpedo. I can teach and describe these things in so much detail that you may *almost* feel it yourself.

But until I strap you into a seat and bring you up into those "footless halls of air,"[9] or get you into waders in Jim Creek in the peak of the Coho run, you will not truly *know* the experience I described.

That is how I feel about discipleship. People told and taught me about discipleship for decades, yet until I experienced it – both being discipled and making disciples – I only knew *about* discipleship. Now, having experienced discipleship, I cannot imagine how I lived without it, and I certainly would not want to go back.

And one reason I don't want to go back is that being discipled and making disciples has completely changed my experience and understanding of suffering because God uses and blesses us powerfully when we are discipled *in* our suffering and when we disciple *from* our suffering.

My Journey of Suffering

All of mankind, Christians or not, are sufferers. It is the nature of our life. While each of us have suffered in different ways, each of

---

[9] John Gillespie Magee, Jr. 1941. "High Flight."

us experience suffering which "is real, tangible, personal, and specific."[10]

Like many of us, I had times of relative freedom from suffering and others of intense immersion in it. I also certainly had times of great personal failure and sin, of struggling to perform to my expectations or those of others, and of the death of dreams. Some of the deeper, harder times of suffering in my life have common themes of loss:

- Our struggle with infertility and the loss of four children before birth.
- The loss through death of family members and all too many friends, many of them military comrades.
- Physical ailments and injuries and corresponding loss of abilities and even identity.
- My wife's now five-year struggle with an aggressive cancer and the effects it has had not only on her health but also on many of our dreams.
- Broken relationships in our family, and the loss of the intimate bonds of trust, care, touch, and even proximity.

It seems strange to have to say this, but all this suffering hurts. It is, as Scott Shaum describes it, an "uninvited companion,"[11] one I wish would leave. Suffering often keeps me up at night, and when I am able to fall asleep, it regularly wakes me up – whether with a back spasm, a nightmare, or a recollection of deep regret. I sometimes feel as if it is all I can do to stand up, much less take the next step. And then at other times, when the suffering seems to have faded into the background, it suddenly jumps back to the forefront or sneaks up on me when I am unaware. I pray often that my suffering will be taken from me.

---

[10] Paul David Tripp, *Suffering: Gospel Hope When Life Doesn't Make Sense*, (Wheaton, IL: Crossway, 2018, 23.
[11] Scott E. Shaum, *The Uninvited Companion: God Shaping Us in His Love through Life's Adversities*, (Middletown, DE: Cresta Riposo, 2017).

While I do not believe all our suffering is a result of spiritual warfare, it is in these times of weakness that I find I am most vulnerable to such attacks. One of the ways the enemy attacks is by trying to isolate me from one of the greatest blessings with which God has gifted me: discipleship.

When I am suffering, I am often tempted to believe two lies: first, that my suffering should be in secret, isolated from those who would disciple me, and second, that my suffering either disqualifies or excuses me from discipling others. But this is the truth I have found: God uses and blesses us powerfully when we are discipled *in* our suffering and when we disciple *from* our suffering.

My Journey of Lament

In 2018, a couple years after becoming a vocational pastor, I took one of Dr. Jim Bruckner's classes, which was largely based on his book, *Healthy Human Life: A Biblical Witness*.[12] In both the class and his book, Bruckner delves deeply into the theology, history, and practice of biblical lament. I was familiar with the term biblical lament, but previously I had not taken the time to understand what it meant, how it was detailed and demonstrated in the Bible, or the power of putting it into practice by, as Bruckner writes:

> *"...speaking to God; by speaking the details of suffering in the presence of others; and by connection to a long tradition of other people who have suffered and found hope in these relationships."*[13]

Over the next years, I began to appreciate the gift of lament, a gift I believe our culture has neglected. I applied it to my own suffering, crying out to God, making my complaints known, trusting in Him for help, and moving into praise, often leading with my head with the hopes my heart would follow. Amidst our culture that

---

[12] James K. Bruckner, *Healthy Human Life: A Biblical Witness*, (Eugene, OR: Cascade, 2012).
[13] Bruckner, 180.

promotes the extremes of either hiding or celebrating suffering without bringing it to the One and only sovereign to address it, I worked to help others practice this discipline in their own hurts, whether in an office counseling session, a pastoral visit, a hospital or hospice room, a funeral, or over a meal with a friend.

Conclusion: Lament as Discipleship

These three journeys on which I am traveling are not separate from each other. They are instead elements of one path the Sovereign God has put before me and ordained before I was born. You are on your own journey that He has similarly ordained, one that will have suffering.[14] For that reason, I hope it also includes discipleship and lament.

Praise be to God that in His lovingkindness He has not called us to walk these trails and trials alone. God Himself is with us, goes before us, guards us from behind, and comes alongside us as we walk along the path to which He has called us, even as we stray from it. In that same lovingkindness, He has given us other travel companions like Jim, Clem, Martha, Mike, and others I will introduce later. As I wrote earlier, our journeys are intertwined with the paths of these companions, helping us to see and follow the Way of Jesus. Then, as we mature in that walk, God calls us to walk alongside and help other fellow travelers. Again, this is discipleship in its most basic form – one person walking alongside another, helping each other grow in Christlikeness.

These journeys also involve peril. We will stumble. We will be attacked. We will be injured and wounded. We will experience loss, grief, discouragement, temptation, and even persecution. We will sin and we will be sinned against. This suffering is promised, has purpose, and like the rest of our journey, is under the sovereignty of God. As our journeys bring us alongside one another, we are called not simply to minister to one another's sufferings, but even to share in them. Our discipleship of others includes both sharing in their troubles – what I will call discipleship *into* suffering, and sharing our

---

[14] Jn 16:33.

troubles with them – discipleship *from* suffering. Both are inseparable from the other aspects of true discipleship, a living out of Scripture's commands to share in both suffering and comfort, and indeed sharing in the sufferings and comforts of Christ Himself.[15]

One of the gifts God gave us to help share His suffering and comfort is the practice of biblical lament. It is "a prayer in pain that leads to trust,"[16] a mourning, or the expression of grief, a natural reaction to suffering and loss, a complaint that speaks to that suffering, addressed to God and designed by Him to be practiced in community. One way we as sufferers are called to come alongside and disciple fellow sufferers, helping them grow in Christlikeness, is through the practice of biblical lament. We help them to cry out to God from their suffering and invite them to lament with us over our own suffering.

Purpose

What This Is Not

As we continue, it is important to consider what this book is *not*. It is not a tutorial on discipleship. There are hundreds of excellent resources on discipleship, and I included some of my favorites in the bibliography. There is always value to recording and reframing the principles and practices of discipleship in a manner that may be more accessible or useful for others, but that is not my purpose in this book. Nor is this a book on suffering. While I will define and describe suffering and the theology of suffering, this is not a deep dive into the topic. There are also plenty of excellent resources on suffering, though probably not as numerous as on discipleship. Again, I included my favorites in the bibliography. I leaned heavily upon several of those both in writing this book and in walking through my own and others' difficult times.

This book also is not an autobiography. I shall continue to use autobiographical vignettes, but I use the stories of others as well. I

---

[15] 2 Co 1:3-7.
[16] Vroegop, Mark, *Dark Clouds, Deep Mercy: Discovering the Grace of Lament*, (Wheaton, IL: Crossway, 2019), 28.

will probably be a bit lopsided in how often I reference cancer, because that is the suffering that occupies much of my lament these days. The purpose of these accounts is not to draw attention to myself or to others, but rather to help readers see themselves in the stories, so my readers may recognize that they are not alone as sufferers called to discipleship.

What This Is

I hope my readers find this a helpful a resource on the relationship between discipleship and suffering, and how biblical lament is vital both in discipleship *into* and discipleship *from* suffering. Rather than a purely scholarly work, it is my desire that the real-life stories told here, combined with the prayerful use of Scripture, will find practical application for fellow sufferers called to disciple and be discipled, again into and from our own suffering and that of others.

To further this end, I will start with a brief discussion to establish a common ground of theology, practice, and terminology, first on discipleship and then on suffering. I will touch upon some of the concepts and practices of discipleship I find useful, some of which might seem familiar to you and some not. I hope my readers find some of these concepts and practices both useful in their contexts and compatible with the other tried-and-tested discipleship principles taught over the past millennia of Jesus growing His Church.

As mentioned earlier, one of the key practices is biblical lament, which I find strangely absent in much of contemporary Christian culture. Consequently, and especially because of its particular usefulness in connecting discipleship with human suffering, I will explore it more than other aspects of discipleship.

From there, we will consider discipleship *into* suffering. What does it look like to disciple a person who is suffering? How can the practices of discipleship, particularly biblical lament, aid us as we come alongside and pour into the life of a fellow sufferer? We will then investigate discipleship *from* suffering. How does God use our suffering to help us disciple others? Can those same practices be used in our own suffering to help form others into Christlikeness?

Discussion

1. As you consider what it would (or does) look like to disciple *into* the suffering of others and *from* your own suffering?
2. What are some significant areas of suffering in your life and in the lives of those you are called to disciple?
3. How would you describe your ministry?

Devotion

Blessed be the God and Father of our Lord Jesus Christ, the Father of mercies and God of all comfort, who comforts us in all our affliction, so that we may be able to comfort those who are in any affliction, with the comfort with which we ourselves are comforted by God. For as we share abundantly in Christ's sufferings, so through Christ we share abundantly in comfort too. If we are afflicted, it is for your comfort and salvation; and if we are comforted, it is for your comfort, which you experience when you patiently endure the same sufferings that we suffer. Our hope for you is unshaken, for we know that as you share in our sufferings, you will also share in our comfort.
- 2nd Corinthians 1:3-7

Lord Jesus, thank you for not only calling us to be disciple-makers, but making us your disciples. Thank you for showing us your loving care as you sought, pursued, embraced, taught, and poured your life into sufferers. Thank you for continuing your work of disciple-making even as you shared in our sufferings and took on even greater suffering for our sakes. Father God, transform us by the power of your Spirit into the likeness of your Son, leading, guiding, encouraging, protecting, and changing us through the afflictions of this life for your name's sake. Amen.

PART 1: SETTING THE STAGE

Discipleship

Defining Discipleship

Jesus' call to follow Him was the call of a rabbi to his disciples, people who sought not only to know what he knows, or even to do what he does, but to be who he is. This kind of call was not to a school or an occupation, because this kind of change could not come through a few lectures every week, or even a full work week. It required the disciple living with the rabbi, seeing not only how he taught, but how he lived his life from his waking hours until he slept. Jesus' method is likewise the rabbinic method: that we would not only grow into his likeness, but pass on that knowledge to others by walking together in an ever-deepening, day-by-day relationship, becoming more like him as we learn from his teaching, his ways, and his presence. This side-by-side, living together, and walking together relationship is the kind of discipleship I hope to define.

I was influenced deeply by the Navigators, where I learned to think of discipleship as a one-on-one relationship, centered on a set curriculum with a heavy emphasis on Scripture memory. Over time, my definition changed somewhat. Similarly, as a person raised in a way that leaned towards the Stoic, I previously tended towards a very narrow definition of suffering. That too has broadened over the years through my own experiences and studying of suffering as well as navigating suffering with others.

> *While walking by the Sea of Galilee, he saw two brothers, Simon (who is called Peter) and Andrew his brother, casting a net into the sea, for they were fishermen. And he said to them, "Follow me, and I will make you fishers of men."*
> *– Matthew 4:18-19*

We could say that almost everything we do as individual Christians and the Church as a whole is discipleship. After all, Jesus said, "Let you light shine before others, so that they may see your good works and give glory to your Father who is in heaven."[17] So even simply living our lives before others has elements of discipleship. Likewise, the weekly sermon, Sunday school, Bible studies, prayer meetings, evangelistic outreaches, service projects, small groups, and discussions over a meal all are means of discipleship and could be an important part of a discipling relationship. However, we are focusing more on discipling relationships than on components of discipleship. For this reason, our working definition for discipleship shall be:

"pouring our lives into intentional, Christ-centered, Scripture-based, prayer-covered, love-soaked relationships with others, helping them know Christ, teaching them obedience to what he has commanded, and growing together in Christlikeness."

This single phrase contains many elements, which we need to consider in greater depth.

Pouring our Lives

Discipleship is intimate and personal. Our model for disciple-making is Jesus Himself, who chose not to teach from afar but to be present, incarnate, living among His disciples, and sharing not only what He knew but who He was. Discipleship is a personal investment, sharing life together with others.

Intentional

Discipleship is not an accident, but is purposeful, deliberate, and planned. This does not imply it is rigid. Flexibility and spontaneity should not only be allowed but encouraged. However, at all times we should remember that there is a purpose for this relationship – to

---

[17] Mt 5:16.

help one another grow in Christlikeness. Aspects of intentionality include regular meetings, focused content and activities, setting goals and milestones, and honest assessments of needs and growth.

Christ-centered

Disciple-makers must always point to Christ. We are not trying to teach people to imitate us, but to imitate us as we imitate Christ, in such a way that they too will be able to teach others our ways in Christ. [18] Discipleship relationships commonly do and should incorporate all aspects of our lives – meals, entertainment, recreation, hobbies, activities, interests, etc. Yet the key distinction separating a discipleship relationship from, say, a book club is that we use the activity (in this case, reading and discussing a book) to point towards Jesus and our growth in Christlikeness.

Scripture-based

God's Word is sufficient to equip us for lives of faith and service, what we need to know to grasp God's Gospel plan to restore our broken relationship with Him through Jesus Christ, to live in that restored relationship with our heavenly Father, and to walk in the ways and perform the works He has prepared for us.[19] Scripture is the critical element of any discipleship relationship because Scripture is the sufficient resource upon which our lives must be founded, and through which the world must be viewed as we grow in Christlikeness. Though Bible study is not the only thing we should do with our disciple or disciple-maker, it must be a significant part of it.

Prayer-covered

"Pray without ceasing"[20] is a high bar that I suggest a very elite few could claim even to approach. Yet God is not shy about setting such high bars. Jesus called us not to be good but said, "You

---

[18] 1 Co 11:1; 4:16-17; 2 Ti 2:2.
[19] 2 Ti 3:16-17.
[20] 1 Th 5:17.

therefore must be perfect, as your heavenly Father is perfect."[21] Praise to Him for His mercy and grace, and for His supply of the Holy Spirit to change us more and more into that perfection. One way He affects said change is by teaching us to rely more and more upon the practice of prayer. Prayer must be a part of our disciple-making meetings, and we should pray for one another before, afterwards, and in the time between. This discipline is one way God can use to move us towards the practice of praying continuously.

Love-Soaked

Our charge as disciples who make disciples is to love them as Jesus loved. It is not only essential to making disciples, but it is essential to our witness of the Gospel to the world.[22] It is this love which binds every aspect of disciple-making "together in perfect harmony."[23] Our disciple-making relationships must be soaked thoroughly in love, the love that is marked by humility, generosity, and a desire for one another's good and growth. As Paul wrote to his disciples in Philippi, "It is right for me to feel this way about you all, because I hold you in my heart... For God is my witness, how I yearn for you all with the affection of Christ Jesus. And it is my prayer that your love may abound more and more..."[24] Our love is not forced, but given, coming from the great love with which Jesus loves us.[25]

Relationships

Relationships are what distinguish discipleship, as we will address it in this book, from disciple-making activities or programs. We can and should learn and grow through sermons, Bible studies, Sunday schools, prayer meetings, and various other ministries and activities that are intentional, Christ-centered, Scripture-based, prayer-covered, and love-soaked. But the people Jesus called His disciples were the ones with whom He lived life in the context of

---

[21] Mt 5:48.
[22] Jn 13:34-35.
[23] Col 3:14.
[24] Phi 1:7a, 8-9.
[25] 1 Jn 3:16.

intimate relationships. While this could include a small group and I hesitate to set an absolute limit on how large a "discipleship group" can be, it is well-established that the smaller a group, the more intimate, transparent, and vulnerable it tends to be. This may be particularly important when we are addressing experiences of suffering.

Teaching Them to Obey all that Christ Commanded

"Why do you call me 'Lord, Lord,' and not do what I tell you?"[26] Here we risk entering into a fray that seems to have become more prominent as of late - legalism vs. antinomianism. I hope to avoid taking either side of this false choice. Jesus included "teaching them to obey [observe] all that I have commanded you"[27] in His most famous summary of discipleship, and emphasized obedience several times elsewhere in His teaching.[28] We teach not only with words but also with our actions, as we bring our speech, thoughts, and indeed our whole bodies into obedience to Christ.[29] As my friend and devoted disciple-maker Ray Bandi teaches, disciple-makers are "models, advocates, and catalysts" for discipleship: **Models** who demonstrate what a disciple of Jesus is through their lives, **Advocates** who speak, write, and urge people to live as intentional, personal disciple-makers, and **Catalysts** who invite people to begin their own journey into disciple-making and personally train them to make other disciples.[30]

Growing Together in Christlikeness

We are each made in the image of God and to be in a relationship with Him.[31] Yet sin tarnishes this image, driving a wedge between us and our loving Creator and separating us from Him with a

---

[26] Lk 6:46.
[27] Mt 28:20.
[28] Mt 7:21; 24-27; Jn 14:21; see also Rom 2:13 and Jas 1:22, among others.
[29] Rom 12:1; Jas 3:1-5.
[30] Ray Bandi, *New England Disciple-Makers Network,* https://www.disciplemakersnetwork.org/ (Accessed August 27, 2023).
[31] Gen 1:26-27.

crevasse so deep we have no hope of crossing it by ourselves. The Bible tells us that in this state we are dead in our sin. But God, in His incomprehensibly rich mercy and great love, makes us alive with Christ through faith in Christ.[32] Having been forgiven and restored, He then calls us to be transformed in this life – conforming not to the world but more and more into the likeness of Jesus Christ.[33] Discipleship is a means through which God has chosen to work this transformation, building up one another so that we will grow up "in every way into him who is the head, into Christ."[34]

Walking in Discipleship

Having defined discipleship, I would like to step back a little bit and establish a wider framework of what it looks like to walk in discipleship, starting with the first example of discipleship we have in Scripture. The first person to pour out His life into an intentional relationship for the purpose of knowing God, being obedient to His commands, and growing in His image, was the triune God of the Bible Himself. And Scripture records Him doing so in the first chapter of the Bible, when God created humans in His image to be in relationship with Him.

Created In the Image of God

As we read the beautiful poetry of creation, the awe - inspiring account of God's powerful sovereignty, it is common to miss the stunning import of God's intentional and purposeful creation of mankind *in His image*. He created us to be His image-bearers so that the earth might be filled with His presence. We are meant to represent Him to the whole of His creation, crowned with glory and honor, and given dominion over the works of His hands.[35]

His made this plan to fill the earth with His image-bearers before the foundation of the world, knowing that we as humans would rebel and stray the call. Jesus Christ, God Himself, came into the world

---

[32] Eph 2:1-10.
[33] Rom 12:2.
[34] Eph 4:11-16.
[35] Ps 8:5-6.

to be the very image of God[36] and empowered us to turn away from the world and grow in Christlikeness as His image-bearers, so that others might come to know Christ and grow in Him as well.[37]

Created in Relationship with God

> *"Someone is watching you right now as you read this. Think about that. The God who loans you life sees your every move, hears each word you speak, and knows your every thought. And this is a good thing. You are seen by God. Noticed. Known." – Francis Chan*[38]

God created us in His image, to be in relationship with Him, and to live with Him in a personal, intimate, face-to-face manner. Do not gloss over this fact. Stop and consider this: You were created to walk with God.

This is something I knew, but I did not stop to consider more deeply until only recently, when I was listening to a lecture by Ed Welch of the Christian Counseling and Educational Foundation (CCEF). Bringing the first three chapters of Genesis together with Isaiah 40 and Micah 6:8, he said, "You are the ideal walking partner for the God who says you are 'very good.'" I stopped the video and listened again, and as I did my eyes drifted to the left side of my laptop, where four hiking maps were set. Earlier that day, I was preparing for a vacation in the mountains in conjunction with my upcoming sabbatical. My wife Martha was coming with me, as were two of our three adult children and another friend who did not yet know Jesus. I was putting great effort and thought into preparing for our walks. I had plans for long and adventurous hikes with grand mountain views and waterfalls. I planned shorter walks for when

---

[36] Col 1:15-17; Heb 1:3.
[37] Jn 17:20-26.
[38] Francis and Lisa Chan, *You and Me Forever: Marriage in Light of Eternity*, (San Francisco, CA: Claire Love Publishing, 2014, 19.

we were tired, and rainy day walks in the adjoining valley. I even planned things to do when Martha, fighting cancer, might not have the energy to do much more than sit and watch the clouds roll by. I'm a dreamer, and so I already imagined how these hikes would look and sound, even how they would smell, feel, and taste. I was saddened that our oldest daughter would not be able to be with us.

And then the understanding hit me.

THE God. The Almighty Creator and King of the universe. *That* God made me to be His ideal walking partner. Before I was born, He planned the path of my life. He planned the hard climbs to mountain summits with breathtaking views. He planned the walks through easy meadows, green pastures, and still waters. He planned the paths that led through the valley of the shadow of death. He planned for the days when I would be too tired or too discouraged or too weak to walk. He planned for the long time I would be separated from Him. He planned the beginning and the end, and while I had vivid images what the paths of our family adventure might be like, God *knows* every detail of my goings up and laying down. And He created me to walk that path with Him.[39]

Job's friend Elihu said to him, "Stop and consider the wondrous works of God."[40] Friend, stop and consider this wondrous work: God created you as His ideal walking partner.

Created for Relationship with Each Other

In the creation account of Genesis, there is a repeated phrase: "And God saw that it was good." The light was good, the Earth and waters were good, the vegetation was good, the Sun, Moon, and stars were good, the living creatures were good. Everything He created was good.[41]

---

[39] Edward T. Welch, "Applied Theology of the Person," Christian Counseling and Education Foundation, 2023, Lecture 3.
[40] Job 37:14.
[41] Gen 1:1-25.

But then He created the first human, and it was here that God saw something in His creation that was not good. God declared, "It is not good that the man should be alone;" and so God created the first human companion, a helper suitable for Him. And after God had created humans in the plural, He saw that it was not only good, but it was "very good."[42]

God in His eternal wisdom, steadfast love, and boundless mercy created us to be in relationship with other humans. These relationships have purpose because two are indeed better than one: we lift one another up when we fall, comfort one another, protect one another, care for one another,[43] and we help one another grow in the knowledge and instruction and even the likeness of our Lord.

While God does speak to individuals in His Scripture, and cares so deeply so as to number the hairs on each person's head,[44] most of Scripture speaks to the plural, to the people rather than the person. We were made to be in community, called not only to know and be known by our God and to worship Him in Spirit and in truth,[45] but also to pass on that knowledge and practice to others as we walk together.[46] This is discipleship, companionship in our journey towards Christlikeness, and it is not a burden but a blessing. It is very good.

Discussion

1. Have you considered what it means to be created by God to walk with Him, not only to know Him but to be known by Him?
2. Is there someone God has put in your life to walk with you to help you grow in Christlikeness? If not, is there someone you could ask to be that person?

---

[42] Gen 1:31; 2:18-25.
[43] Ecc 4:9-12.
[44] Lk 12:7.
[45] Jn 4:24.
[46] Dt 6:1-25; 2 Ti 2:2.

3. Who has God put before you to help grow in Christ?

Devotion

> You then, my child, be strengthened by the grace that is in Christ Jesus, and what you have heard from me in the presence of many witnesses entrust to faithful men, who will be able to teach others also. Share in suffering as a good soldier of Christ Jesus. No soldier gets entangled in civilian pursuits, since his aim is to please the one who enlisted him. An athlete is not crowned unless he competes according to the rules. It is the hard-working farmer who ought to have the first share of the crops. Think over what I say, for the Lord will give you understanding in everything.
>
> Remember Jesus Christ, risen from the dead, the offspring of David, as preached in my gospel, for which I am suffering, bound with chains as a criminal. But the word of God is not bound! Therefore, I endure everything for the sake of the elect, that they also may obtain the salvation that is in Christ Jesus with eternal glory. The saying is trustworthy, for:

If we have died with him, we will also live with him;
if we endure, we will also reign with him;
if we deny him, he also will deny us;
if we are faithless, he remains faithful—
for he cannot deny himself.
– 2nd Timothy 2:1-13

Suffering

Introduction

> *"Coming to Christ means more suffering, not less, in this world. I am persuaded that suffering is normal and not exceptional. We all will suffer; we all must suffer; and most American Christians are not prepared in mind or heart to believe or experience this. Therefore, the glory of God, the honor of Christ, the stability of the church, and the strength of commitment to world missions are at stake. If our conversations do not help people become satisfied in God through suffering, then God will not be glorified, Christ will not be honored, the church will be a weakling in an escapist world of ease, and the completion of the Great Commission with its demand for martyrdom will fail."*
> *– John Piper*[47]

Suffering is the condition or experience of physical, emotional, psychological, and/or spiritual discomfort, pain, or distress, regardless of intensity, duration, or cause. It is diverse in its nature and normative in this life. It can vary in intensity and cause. It is the root of some of our most difficult questions regarding the goodness and sovereignty of God, questions that can only be answered satisfactorily if we conclude that suffering is not meaningless, but has purposes that demonstrate God's sovereignty, mercy, and work in its midst.

---

[47] John Piper, "Counseling with Suffering People," *DesiringGod*. February 1, 2003. https://www.desiringgod.org/articles/counseling-with-suffering-people.

The Nature of Suffering

"What?" Suffering is Diverse

> *"Suffering in the modern world is readily associated with experiences that sometimes overlap one another — physical, emotional or psychological pain. However experienced, pain and suffering often are inseparable."*
> *– H.A. Thomas*[48]

Suffering comes in many forms. Every one of us suffers differently. We suffer through loss, grief, pain, and hurt. That injury can come in many realms, physical, emotional, psychological, moral, spiritual, relational, and even financial. Indeed, for any conceivable category of well-being, we can likely imagine (or not need to imagine) a corresponding form of suffering. We experience a wide assortment of suffering including illness, failure, shame, entrapment and consequences of addiction, death of loved ones and of dreams, sorrow of broken relationships and lost opportunities, and most tragically, the ultimate and terrible suffering that awaits those who remain apart from God's saving grace. As John Piper put it, we must "care about all human suffering, especially eternal suffering. Else they have a defective heart or a flameless hell."[49]

"Who and Where?" Suffering is Normative

As you read the last paragraph, you likely recalled specific experiences you could attach to the various forms of suffering. You and/or a loved one may have lived or are living through this hurt. Suffering is a normative part of our life in this world. This should

---

[48] H. A. Thomas, "Suffering," in Boda, Mark J. and McConville, Gordon J., Eds. *Dictionary of the Old Testament: Prophets*, (Downers Grove, IL: IVP Academic, 2012), 757.

[49] Andy Johnson, *Missions: How the Local Church Goes Global*, (Wheaton, IL: Crossway, 2017), 22.

not surprise us, says Jesus. "In the world you will have tribulation."[50] Later, Peter devotes much of his first letter to suffering, instructing his readers, "Beloved, do not be surprised at the fiery trial when it comes upon you to test you, as though something strange were happening to you."[51] Throughout both the Old and New Testaments, we see that suffering was and should be expected to be the norm, not the exception, and even ordained by the God who makes both light and darkness, well-being and calamity.[52]

"How Much?" The Intensity of Suffering

I have met few true Stoics, but many of us have been influenced by the philosophy at least to some extent. We are tempted to minimize or dismiss our suffering and that of others as minor, inconsequential, irrelevant, or even non-existent. When we do acknowledge it, we rightfully see that suffering varies not only in type but also in intensity, an intensity that is hard to quantify and may be different depending on perspective.

Of course, all suffering is not equal in severity. As I wrote today, a toddler cried out in pain after he fell backwards and hit his head lightly on the floor. It would be foolish to claim that his suffering equaled that of the woman seated next to me in the café, whose head was wrapped in bandages with steel apparatus coming out from her skull. Nor could we equate that suffering with the student at another table who is frustrated by an assignment she is working on. We also cannot compare that with the suffering caused by the fires in Hawaii where hundreds of people are dead or missing and thousands homeless, or that of the hundreds of thousands without power and in danger of losing homes in the hurricane battering Florida, or of the millions who have been displaced, wounded, or killed in the past year alone in wars raging in Sudan, Ukraine, Myanmar, Gaza, and Ethiopia, and multiple smaller wars being

---

[50] Jn 16:33b.
[51] 1 Pet 4:12.
[52] Dt 8:3; Job 1-41; Ps 34:19; Is 45:7; Mt 10:38; Rom 8:18; 2 Co 1:3-4; 4:17; Phi 1:29; 3:10…

waged across the world. It would be foolish to try to compare the severity of these sufferings.

While all suffering is not equal, it is all suffering – whether it is the suffering of the hurt toddler or the widowed war refugee. Because of the universal aspect of suffering – that all of us suffer – we can all relate to sufferers. Even more beautifully, Jesus Himself not only suffered and entered into the suffering of others but did both intentionally and purposefully. We are united to one another and to Jesus in suffering.

"Why?" The Causes of Suffering

There are diverse causes of suffering. Sometimes these causes are easy to discern. Several years ago, I suffered fractures of ribs and vertebrae. The cause wasn't difficult to discern. In my foolishness and haste while retrieving runaway horses, I decided to ride one of them back to the stable bareback on the ice, and when the unshod horse predictably lost his footing on an icy sloped driveway, he likewise predictably jolted. With only a handful of mane to steady myself, I very predictably upended and fell to the ground! More often, the causes of suffering are more difficult to see or understand. And frequently, our pride leads us to believe we know the cause or causes when we really do not. Therefore, we oftentimes respond poorly to our own suffering and that of others. Related to this common error is our tendency, and even our deep desire, to seek simple answers to causality when the truth is usually much more complex. If you dare, you might observe support for this theory at your next gathering with friends or family were you to ask, "what causes _____?" In the blank, you may insert words like "fentanyl addiction," "illiteracy," "child abuse," "homelessness," "divorce," or just about any other type of suffering imaginable.

"How Can It Be?" Suffering and Theodicy

Suffering inevitably brings us to the question of theodicy: how can it be that the suffering coexists with a loving, merciful, just, omniscient, and omnipotent God? Many answer this question by asserting that the foundational assumptions of this question are wrong, that God is cruel, indifferent, unjust, unknowing, and/or impotent in the face of suffering. Some religions and philosophies also attack the question by asserting that suffering doesn't exist except as a human construct and response to circumstances that are themselves amoral. Yet Scripture teaches differently, emphasizing that God is simultaneously sovereign, severe, just, knowing, loving, and merciful, and that there is purpose and goodness behind the suffering He allows and even ordains.

Suffering Is Not Meaningless

> *He has made everything beautiful in its time. Also, he has put eternity into man's heart, yet so that he cannot find out what God has done from the beginning to the end.*
> *– Ecclesiastes 3:11*

> *"You must know two things about God. You must know God has brought this suffering to you. You must know that He is wise enough, that He did not flinch, but decreed everything that has ever come into your life. He's strong. He's powerful. And He has His own agenda. But you must also know that this God is also compassionate beyond our describing. He's tender. He's merciful beyond what any mother could be. God who is strong and runs the world, whose compassion interlaces everything, this God is the true God."*
> *– Joni Eareckson-Tada*[53]

While sometimes God in His mercy and kindness allows us to see some of His purposes behind suffering, to think we are able to grasp the entirety of them this side of heaven is to misunderstand the gulf

---

[53] Steve Estes and Joni Eareckson Tada, "Which God is in Your Sufferings?" *The Journal of Biblical Counseling*, 2004, 23.

between our thoughts and purposes and those of the Almighty and unsearchable God.[54] In fact, it is not only arrogant but also often hurtful to assume that we do know the complete answers to these difficult questions regarding the suffering. Yet we do know some general truths for all human suffering: that God is merciful in it, sovereign over it, and has purpose in it. These truths are inseparable, yet we usually favor one while shunning or at least neglecting the others.

God is Merciful in Our Suffering

> *You have heard of the steadfastness of Job,*
> *and you have seen the purpose of the Lord,*
> *how the Lord is compassionate and merciful.*
> *– James 5:11*

One day one day I found myself sitting across from Nick Clark, a man who was my confidant, counselor, and dear friend. In other words, Nick was a disciple-maker. As I sat on the sofa in his office, I averted my eyes and took in the titles of the books on his shelf while answering a question I no longer remember. I was in pain. My wife was – as she still is – fighting cancer. I had really blown it as a father. I was struggling and losing the fight against my sin of anger. I was carrying the loads of my own flock; deaths, losses, struggles, brokenness, and sin. I was sad. I was depressed. I had lost a good bit of hope. And I don't know if I even answered his question.

Then, Nick asked another question. And it seemed off-base... off-topic. But, of course, it was not.

"Pat, do you know that God is kind?"

"Yes, of course."

"No. Do you know that God is *kind*?" Not just good. Not just righteous. Not just generous. "Do you know that God. Is. Kind?"

---

[54] Is 55:8.

I stopped and thought and contemplated and realized the truth. I knew in my mind that God was kind, but I did not believe it in my heart. I realized that deep down, my concept of God was lopsided – a wonderful, awesome, majestic, righteous, powerful, pure, glorious King and Creator. But I did not fully embrace the fact that He is also the one who says He is gentle and lowly in heart, patient, loving, caring, and yes, kind. I knew that this righteous God reaches out to us even in our sinfulness, sending Jesus, God the Son, to live among us, suffer and die in our place for our sins, and then defeat sin and death by rising again so that those who truly believe and receive the gift might be forgiven of those sins and live with Him eternally. Somehow though, I missed out in trusting that this salvation pointed to an elemental, essential, undeniable yet indescribable truth about God's nature. It is only *because* of His *kindness* that He could embrace us, redeem us, and save us. Thus I realized that in my heart of hearts, I did not embrace this truth: that God is kind.

When Moses asked God to show him His glory, God responded by passing before him and proclaiming His name. Not His label, but His name – what God is called because of who He is. God's proclamation had two major components: His merciful love and His righteous power. He led with the former: "The LORD, the LORD, a God merciful and gracious, slow to anger, and abounding in steadfast love and faithfulness, keeping steadfast love for thousands, forgiving iniquity and transgression and sin..."[55]

Repeated twice is the Hebrew word חֶסֶד (*hesed*), translated in various English versions as "steadfast love," "unfailing love," "longsuffering," "mercy," "loyal love," and "lovingkindness." When God tells the person who will lead, care for, and teach His people, He starts by telling him of His compassion, grace, patience, lovingkindness, truth, and forgiveness. In my head I knew this to be true, but my heart was having difficulty grasping it.

Over the next years before his death, Nick taught both my head and my heart, not just with words, but with true shepherding, true

---

[55] Exo 34:6-7a.

pastoring, and true discipleship. He taught me God was kind by being a kind friend, by showing kindness to others, and by partnering with me in pastoring my congregation. He taught me God was kind by helping me do barn chores, including wrestling and tattooing goats, when my wife couldn't help. He taught me God was kind by being humble and letting me serve him. He taught me God was kind by always greeting me with the type of hug that only a guy like Nick could give (he was 6'8", with shoulders and arms to match). Most importantly, he taught me God was kind by echoing Paul's words to Timothy – "Imitate me as I imitate Christ."

God is kind. He is merciful. He is the one who heals the brokenhearted and binds up their wounds, the one to whom we in our suffering can cry out, "Abba! Father!"[56]

God Is Sovereign in Our Suffering

"Do you know the balancings of the clouds,
the wondrous works of him who is perfect in
knowledge,
you whose garments are hot
when the earth is still because of the south
wind?"
– Job 37:16-17

We need to know God is merciful in our suffering. However, if that is all to which we grasp, we may find ourselves agreeing with Rabbi Harold Kushner's book, *When Bad Things Happen to Good People*, in which he incorrectly concluded that because of God's overwhelming kindness, He could not possibly want us to suffer, and therefore suffering must be out of God's ability to control. Such an image of God is comforting and easy to accept, at least at first. Yet "A God like this, who is only like this, who allows this world to get out of hand like He does, must be a God who cannot do more. In the

---

[56] Ps 147:3; Rom 8:15.

end, this compassionate-only God cannot be a satisfying God. He cannot quench the thirst of a suffering person."[57]

God's matchless mercy only makes sense in light of His matchless sovereignty. It may be tempting to focus only upon the vastness of His mercy and lovingkindness and the comfort that they bring, giving rightful praise and thanksgiving for His provision and care in our suffering. It is altogether more difficult for many of us to grasp that God is sovereign in that same suffering, for then we must accept that God not only allows suffering but even ordains it. How can this be? This is a question that has befuddled even the Preacher of Ecclesiastes, who declared "Vanity of vanities... all is vanity."[58]

Yet it is true. God is sovereign in our suffering. He says it Himself.

> *"I form light and create darkness;*
> *I make well-being and create calamity;*
> *I am the LORD who does all these things."*
> *– Isaiah 45:7*

The all-powerful God of all creation, in His sovereignty, ordains light and darkness, well-being and calamity, as He works all things according to the counsel of His will, to the praise of His glory.[59]

We see this illustrated powerfully in the book of Job, where Satan makes great accusations against God's sovereignty – claiming first that God doesn't understand Job's motives by asserting that Job's fear of God is transactional and conditional upon God's protection of Job's family, possessions, work, and wealth. In a move that offends our senses and perhaps surprises not only Satan but also the witnesses in the heavenly court, God calls Satan's bluff by handing His righteous servant Job over to the adversary to suffer. We who read this account have our doubts about God's sovereignty, His goodness, or both. How could a perfectly good, all-powerful God

---

[57] Estes and Tada, 22.
[58] Eccl 12:8.
[59] Eph 1:11-12.

throw Job into a high-stakes contest as if he were only a stack of poker chips?

But if we truly believe in God's sovereignty, we realize that God isn't gambling with Job at all, because God never has uncertainty and thus never gambles or takes risks. God knew Job, God ordained the contest and the rules under which it was held, and God knew the outcome before the contest even started.

This concept of God ordaining suffering in both His limitless sovereignty and His limitless mercy can only be true if that suffering has purposes that align with both of these attributes. Praise to our merciful and sovereign God that this is true!

God Is Changing Us In and Through Our Suffering

> *And we all, with unveiled face, beholding the glory of the Lord, are being transformed into the same image from one degree of glory to another. For this comes from the Lord who is the Spirit.*
> *– 2nd Corinthians 3:18*

> *"We must build into our minds and hearts a vision of God and his ways that help us see suffering not merely as a threat to our satisfaction in God (which it is), but also as a means to our satisfaction in God (which it is). We must talk so as to make suffering seem normal and purposeful, and not surprising in this fallen age."*
> *- John Piper*[60]

Because of His sovereignty, and because of His great compassion, God is working through our relationship with Jesus, our

---

[60] Piper (2003).

relationships with others, and through circumstances, including our suffering, to change us from one degree of glory to another, continually molding us more into His image. "He is always enabling us to grow amid the difficulties of our situation. While we don't always respond well, he is always at work through his Spirit, convicting us and turning our hearts back to him for the help we need."[61]

> *Thus says the Lord:*
> *"Cursed is the man who trusts in man*
> *and makes flesh his strength,*
> *whose heart turns away from the Lord.*
>
> *He is like a shrub in the desert,*
> *and shall not see any good come.*
> *He shall dwell in the parched places of the wilderness,*
> *in an uninhabited salt land.*
>
> *"Blessed is the man who trusts in the Lord,*
> *whose trust is the Lord.*
>
> *He is like a tree planted by water,*
> *that sends out its roots by the stream,*
> *and does not fear when heat comes,*
> *for its leaves remain green,*
> *and is not anxious in the year of drought,*
> *for it does not cease to bear fruit."*
> *– Jeremiah 17:5-8*

David Powlison, the late Executive Director of the Christian Counseling and Education Foundation (CCEF), developed a model of biblical change based upon Jeremiah 17:5-8. The illustration is of

---

[61] Andrew Nichols and Helen Thorne, *Real Change: Becoming More Like Jesus in Everyday Life*, (Greensboro, NC: New Growth Press, 2018), 17.

two trees, one dying in the wastelands and another flourishing near a stream. Both are under the same stresses – the heat of the sun baking the earth. The chief difference lies in where their roots extend. The Father sends the Spirit to redirect the roots of our hearts from the tainted soil of the world to the richness of Christ and His completed work on the cross. As those changed roots then draw from that living water, the Spirit changes our hearts, and this leads to the ultimate purpose: not a change of circumstance but changed lives and changed fruit.[62]

While I do not know the specific purposes of my own specific sufferings, much less yours or anyone else's, I do know this: God is using our suffering for His purposes, and according to the counsel of His perfect will, and one of these purposes is to change us from one degree of glory to another, transforming us into Christlikeness.

Discussion

1. What have been the formative instances or seasons of suffering in your life?
2. Which is easier for you to see in your suffering: God's mercy, sovereignty, or purpose? Which is harder?
3. How does the knowledge that God is perfect in His mercy, sovereignty, and purposes change your perception of your suffering?

Devotion

PSALM 6: TO THE CHOIRMASTER: WITH STRINGED INSTRUMENTS; ACCORDING TO THE SHEMINITH. A PSALM OF DAVID.

*O LORD, rebuke me not in your anger,
nor discipline me in your wrath.*

---

[62] For an excellent six-week study on this concept, see (Nichols, Andrew and Thorne, Helen 2018). CCEF also offers an online version of the full *Dynamics of Biblical Change* course created by Powlison which takes a deep dive into this process – www.ccef.org.

Be gracious to me, O LORD, for I am languishing;
heal me, O LORD, for my bones are troubled.
My soul also is greatly troubled.
But you, O LORD—how long?

Turn, O LORD, deliver my life;
save me for the sake of your steadfast love.
For in death there is no remembrance of you;
in Sheol who will give you praise?

I am weary with my moaning;
every night I flood my bed with tears;
I drench my couch with my weeping.
My eye wastes away because of grief;
it grows weak because of all my foes.

Depart from me, all you workers of evil,
for the LORD has heard the sound of my weeping.
The LORD has heard my plea;
the LORD accepts my prayer.
All my enemies shall be ashamed and greatly troubled;
they shall turn back and be put to shame in a moment.

Biblical Lament

Introduction: The Gift of Biblical Lament

> *PSALM 13: TO THE CHOIRMASTER. A PSALM OF DAVID.*
>
> *How long, O Lord? Will you forget me forever?*
> *How long will you hide your face from me?*
> *How long must I take counsel in my soul*
> *and have sorrow in my heart all the day?*
> *How long shall my enemy be exalted over me?*
>
> *Consider and answer me, O Lord my God;*
> *light up my eyes, lest I sleep the sleep of death,*
> *lest my enemy say, "I have prevailed over him,"*
> *lest my foes rejoice because I am shaken.*
>
> *But I have trusted in your steadfast love;*
> *my heart shall rejoice in your salvation.*
>
> *I will sing to the Lord,*
> *because he has dealt bountifully with me.*

Biblical lament "a prayer in pain that leads to trust."[63] Using Psalm 13 as a model of "biblical lament in miniature," we can see that lament:

- Assures us that we are in a long line of those who have lamented
- Addresses God as the One who can answer our cries

---

[63] Vroegop, 28.

- Presents our complaints honestly and openly to God
- Expresses trust in God's sovereignty, mercy, and faithfulness
- Commits to praise God in the midst of our suffering

"Western culture, in general, does not grieve well. In fact, most of us have few models of grief well-journeyed. We attend a loved one's funeral and the funeral home is, well, sterile and quiet. If there are tears, they are stifled as others scramble for the tissue box, saying, 'There, there, everything is going to be all right.'"
– *Scott Shaum*[64]

Biblical lament offends such sensibilities. It is a raw cry of grief, a cry that complains about our suffering to the One who hears. However, while all lament is complaint, all complaint is not lament, and all lament is not biblical lament. "Everyone who suffers laments, but not all lament leads to hope."[65]

Lament, not Complaint

Simply addressing a complaint to God does not make it biblical lament. Instead, it presents the danger of being an allegation against God, accusing Him of injustice and, as Bruce Waltke warns, "reduces 'I AM' to a god whose sense of social justice is being questioned like an accused criminal in the dock! It pushes the limits of what it is to be human to being as gods. It legitimizes the voice of blasphemy."[66] What Waltke is saying in this is that mere complaint to God can be an accusation against God's character and his nature. In no manner do we wish to join in this practice. Rather, we must find the defining line between the unrighteousness of the created shaking of our fists against our Creator, which He condemns,[67] and telling truth in suffering to our loving Father, which He welcomes. "If Jesus can lament to his Father in heaven about something he does

---

[64] Shaum, 101.
[65] Bruckner, 181.
[66] Bruce K. Waltke, *The Psalms as Christian Lament*, (Grand Rapids, MI: Eerdmans, 2014), 1.III.
[67] Job 1:1-2

obediently and without sin, can we not also bring our deepest feelings to the one who already knows them?"[68]

What sets biblical lament apart from common complaint is that while complaint centers upon the suffering and/or the sufferer, biblical lament "is centered in *laments of the afflicted directed toward God within the community of faith.*"[69] It is a cry of pain that recognizes the One who can heal, and in that cry and recognition, humbly acknowledges that sufferers are subservient to the Creator and Healer. James Bruckner defines lament as "*a therapeutic monologue of complaint toward God.*" Therapeutic in that it is part of the healing process which gives the lamenter a voice with God, a monologue that is not challenged and instead "allowed to stand as the expression of the sufferer's suffering," and is directed toward God in a desire to re-enter a healed and whole relationship with that Creator and Healer.[70]

God Welcomes Lament

While our culture often **ignores, silences,** or **isolates** the lamenter, denying the therapeutic effects of biblical lament,[71] we are blessed to have a God who shows no propensity to do this. Rather, we see throughout the Bible that God **hears** and **encourages** lament, and that the process of biblical lament, rather than isolating the lamenter, actually **draws the person closer to a restored relationship with God.** After losing his children and his property, Job lamented. He arose, expressed his grief by tearing his robe, shaving his head, and falling on the ground, and then cried out to God, worshipping. "Naked I came from my mother's womb and naked I shall return. The LORD gave, and the LORD has taken away; blessed be the name of the LORD." Scripture says, "in all this Job did not sin..."[72] Instead, we see the elements of biblical lament within our definition above. It is the lament of the afflicted, directed toward

---

[68] (Bruckner 2012, 183).
[69] *Ibid*, 181.
[70] *Ibid*, 181-182.
[71] *Ibid*, 181.
[72] Job 1:13-22

God, and within the community of faith (his wife and messenger-servants at the minimum). It is a cry of complaint to God that acknowledges the suffering, while expressing trust in and praise to the Lord.[73]

Lament is described throughout the Bible for various sufferings. In the Old Testament, it is perhaps David who most of us would add to Job as examples of this practice. David writes several psalms of lament as he flees the persecution of Saul and others, including his own son, Absalom. In these psalms we see him crying out to God in grief, praying for relief, putting his trust in God, and worshipping the Lord.

> *I am weary with my moaning;*
> *every night I flood my bed with tears;*
> *I drench my couch with my weeping.*
> *My eye wastes away because of grief;*
> *it grows weak because of all my foes.*
> *– Psalm 6:9*

> *Deliver me from my enemies, O my God;*
> *protect me from those who rise up against me;*
> *deliver me from those who work evil,*
> *and save me from bloodthirsty men.*
> *- Psalm 59:1-2*

---

[73] This structure is found throughout the psalms, over one third of which are laments (Waltke 2014, 1.I.). It is clearly and concisely illustrated through Psalm 13, the shortest of those laments. It is a psalm which "is a prayer for help by one who in his distress feels forsaken by God (verse 1) and yet rejoices, trusting in his love (verses 5-6). Such is the constant dilemma of faith, fully exemplified in Christ's cry of dereliction on the cross (Matt. 27: 46) and reflected in the joyous praise of his saints amidst unspeakable suffering (cp. Acts 16: 22-6; Rom. 5: 3)." (Rojerson, J.W. and McKay, J.W. 1977, 58).

Sometimes his words might seem demanding, accusing, and even impetuous:

> *Answer me when I call, O God of my righteousness!*
> *– Psalm 4:1*

> *My soul also is greatly troubled.*
> *But you, O LORD – how long?*
> *– Psalm 6:3*

> *Why, O LORD, do you stand far away?*
> *Why do you hide yourself in times of trouble?*
> *– Psalm 10:1*

Yet God does not strike him down, rebuke him, nor condemn him for his raw words. Rather, He calls David "a man after his own heart."[74] As with Job's cries, God does not recoil from these hard questions and guttural cries. Rather, it appears He draws closer.

The psalmist Asaph shows that lament is not the sole purview or privilege of kings.

> *I cry aloud to God,*
> *aloud to God, and he will hear me.*
> *In the day of my trouble I seek the LORD;*
> *in the night my hand is stretched out without wearying;*
> *my soul refuses to be comforted.*
> *When I remember God, I moan;*
> *when I meditate, my spirit faints. Selah.*

> *You hold my eyelids open;*
> *I am so troubled that I cannot speak…*

---

[74] 1 Sa 13:14; Acts 13:22.

> *...Has God forgotten to be gracious?*
> *Has he in anger shut up his compassion?*
> *Selah*
> *— Psalm 77:1-4, 9*

Later, the prophets like Joel call on the God's people and their leaders to lament for how they have fallen away from God, to repent in their grief.

> *Put on sackcloth and lament, O priests;*
> *wail, O ministers of the altar.*
> *Go in, pass the night in sackcloth,*
> *O ministers of God!*
> *Because grain offering and drink offering*
> *are withheld from the house of your God.*
> *Consecrate a fast;*
> *call a solemn assembly.*
> *Gather the elders*
> *and all the inhabitants of the land*
> *to the house of the LORD your God,*
> *and cry out to the LORD.*
> *— Joel 1:13-4*

Neither is lament solely an Old Testament practice. Jesus ends a parable by saying, "And will not God give justice to his elect, who cry to him day and night?"[75] Jesus also tells His own disciples that they will lament His death.[76] Indeed, Jesus Himself cries out while deeply moved and in great distress, both over the death of Lazarus and His own upcoming persecution and execution.[77]

---

[75] Lk 18:7.
[76] Jn 16:20.
[77] Jn 11:35-38; Mt 26:38-44.

A Neglected Gift

Yet biblical lament remains one of the many gifts we neglect and fail to appreciate. Bruce Waltke writes that "it is obvious that 'lament' and 'confession' are not central features of our Western Christian life today. Rather a 'programmatic' and pragmatic view of Christian action prevails, reflecting the secular attitude around us."[78] While lament was quite common in the cultures of both the Old and New Testaments, Nathaniel Carlson notes that in the 950 themes which the popular *SongSelect* software uses to categorize worship music, "lament" is absent, as are "pain" and "suffering."[79]

If you reflect on the last several worship services in which you participated, you are unlikely to recall singing, whether an older hymn or more modern song, about crying out to God in our suffering. During a preaching series on the book of Job, I found the sermon on chapter 3, when Job reaches the depth of his pain, to be perhaps the most difficult to write. As I prepared, I knew I was in good company, having read this excerpt from a commentary:

"The third chapter of Job must be one of the most depressing chapters in the Bible. While some might be as depressed as Job was and use these verses to give vent to their feelings, few sermons are made from this chapter, few verses are claimed as promises, and few are remembered for the warmth of their sentiment. It is the lowest of several low points in the book and seems to counter the high faith of 1:21 and 2:10."[80]

"Few sermons are made from this chapter" indeed. As I completed my outline, I searched for other sermons by trusted preachers to see if they arrived at similar conclusions. I discovered that the commentary was correct. Very few sermons, at least of late, come from this chapter. Two sermons by one pastor looked

---

[78] Waltke, 1.II.
[79] Nathaniel A. Carlson, "Lament: The Biblical Language of Trauma," *Cultural Encounters*, 11, No 1 (January, 2015), 53.
[80] Robert L. Alden, *Job*, (Nashville, TN: Broadman & Holman Publishers, 1993), 71.

promising. In each of them, chapter 3 was covered in only three sentences. I was excited when I found a sermon on Job 3 from a congregation whose pastoral team I hold in high regard. A full minute of an hour-long sermon exegeted chapter 3, and the rest of the message focused on what many would call the "more redemptive" parts of the book. The only in-depth sermon I found on this chapter was written 140 years ago by Charles Spurgeon, focusing on verse 23.[81]

There is a reason. Alden is overly generous when he writes that "few verses are claimed as promises, and few are remembered for the warmth of their sentiment." You will not find them on refrigerator magnets. After two chapters of seeing Satan shamed and God glorified, of good triumphing over evil, we come to a chapter that seems to be true despair, devoid of hope.

However, as I continued working on that sermon, I discovered that gloomy though this passage may be, Job's descent into despair begins to point Job towards true hope. It is a hope that proves that despair, like Satan its father, is a liar. Chapter 3, uncomfortable, raw, rough, and even crude as it is, marks the turning point of Job's descent. In that absolute depth of his despair is where he cries out to God and then makes his complaint. Job 3 differs from the "complete" laments we find in many of the psalms. It is a lament, yet one which is incomplete and unsatisfying. Job cries out in despair, curses the day of his birth, asks questions which cannot be answered, and longs for death. What is missing, however, is the trust *in* and praise *of* God. We will see glimpses of that in the next 39 chapters,[82] but it will not come to fruition until the end of the book when Job returns to trust and worship of God.[83] This is the critical first stage in this practice, to acknowledge that even if we are in despair, that we can – we must – cry out to God, for He is the only one who can both hear and act. It is what a dear friend described as

---

[81] Charles H. Spurgeon, "A Sorrowful Man's Question," *Spurgeon Gems*, (Oct 8, 1882), https://www.spurgeongems.org/sermon/chs2666.pdf.
[82] Job 19:25-27, for instance.
[83] Job 42:1-6.

"coming to God and staying at the table with Him and talking with Him and engaging with Him through the process."[84]

An Exclusive Gift

While all humanity experiences pain, suffering, and affliction, the gift of biblical lament is available only to those who rely upon the one true God. "Lament is a prayer in pain that leads to trust."[85]

Lament is a mourning, or the expression of grief, a natural reaction to suffering and loss, a complaint that speaks to that suffering. Biblical lament addresses that cry to God, seeking to draw near to Him, and the privilege to do so comes only to those who put their faith in Him, who "believe that he exists and that he rewards those who seek him."[86] While all will one day bow down before the sovereignty of the King of the Universe,[87] it is only the children of that King who have the privilege of entering His chambers, drawing near to Him, climbing up on His lap, and weeping on His shoulder.[88]

So why do we neglect a gift such as this, a privilege reserved only for the children of the King?

One reason is that we are afraid to acknowledge how weak our faith is, and how much hope we have lost. If this is the case for you, I ask you to return with me to Job's misery in chapter 3. You probably heard a cry similar to Job's. You may have cried out in the same way yourself. "I wish I had never been born." "There is no hope." "The world would be better off without me." "I would be better off dead." "I wish I would just die." Some of us may have been deceived so deeply by the lies of despair that we have tried to bring this cry to reality by our own hands.

---

[84] Nicholas J. Clark, "An Uncomfortable Psalm: A Sermon on Psalm 77," (Loudon, NH: Faith Community Bible Church, Nov 12, 2021)..
[85] (Vroegop 2019, 28).
[86] Heb 11:6.
[87] Phi 2:10.
[88] Mt 11:28-30; Jn 1:12.

We are tempted to look at Job, stricken, in pain, in misery, crying out from the ashes, and say "he has lost all hope." But as awful as Job's situation is, as deep as his suffering is, he has not yet given up hope. Complete hopelessness, total despair, would find Job not crying out but curled up in a corner waiting to die.

As awfully gut-wrenching as cries like Job's are, like yours are, like ours are, I believe that these cries show that a sliver of hope remains because **the cry of hopelessness still has the hope that someone will hear.** We cry out in anguish in the hopes that someone will hear, that someone will answer, that someone will help.

Cry out to God. Tell Him your deepest struggles, your loss of hope, your weakness of faith. Cry out to Him like the weak-faithed father cried to Jesus: "I believe; help my unbelief!"[89] Knock on the Father's door and find it is opened to you. Enter into His presence, or simply cry out in the darkness. Call on Him. Draw near to Him. Fall into His lap. Fall into His arms. Weep. Mourn. Lament.

Lament in Miniature

What does a "complete" biblical lament look like? Bruckner uses Psalm 13 as an example of this practice in miniature, its six short verses illustrating the basic components and principles of biblical lament. He notes that the superscript of the psalm, "A Psalm of David," (which is part of the original Hebrew Scriptures) is of critical importance as it reminds us **we are in a long line of biblical lamenters**. It points to the fact that we are not alone in lamenting.[90] Lament at times is intensely personal, yet even the some Psalms categorized as "individual laments" often include instructions to the choirmaster or as to specific instruments, indicating that these were to be expressed in corporate worship.[91] Moreover, this superscript reminds us as lamenters that we are in good company. David was also a lamenter, and God called him "a man after his own heart."[92]

---

[89] Mk 9:24.
[90] Bruckner, 184.
[91] Carlson, 59.
[92] 1 Samuel 13:14; Acts 13:22

From here, Bruckner details an outline of biblical lament within the psalm:

1. **Address and petition to the LORD (vv 1-3a):** Biblical lament is, of course, directed to our God, the Lord. The first verse opens by doing so. "How long, O LORD?" This address focuses the cry to the Lord as the one to whom we pray,[93] acknowledges that the Lord hears those cries when we pray to Him,[94] and acknowledges our faith in Him, "for whoever would draw near to God must believe that he exists and that he rewards those who seek him."[95] So, while David cries out in his suffering in verses 1-3a, "his reason and his faith encourage him to offer his prayer and expect a response, trusting that God has not completely withdrawn."[96]

2. **Complaint describing our distress and request for help (vv 3b-4):** David describes the perceived consequences of suffering and makes a plea for help. These cries are unrestrained and speak to the desolation and despair that David feels. It matters not if he will actually be overcome, fall, and die, but that the "real and imagined alienation of the one who is suffering"[97] is David's perceived reality. "He refuses to tell God what he thinks God wants to hear. Rather, he is honest."[98] Lament fights the heresy that the faithful Christian life is one only of happiness with the absence of sadness. On the contrary, "joy is the last word, but lament may fill much of a Christian's earthly sufferings."[99] In fact, we see in the Bible not only that suffering and tribulation is

---

[93] Psalm 5:2
[94] Psalm 4:3
[95] Hebrews 11:6
[96] J.W. Rojerson and J.W. McKay, *The Cambridge Bible Commentary on the New English Bible: Psalms 1-50*, (Cambridge: Cambridge University Press, 1977), 59.
[97] Bruckner, 184.
[98] Glen E. Harris, Jr., "A Wounded Warrior Looks at Psalm 13," *The Journal of Pastoral Theology*, 2010, 2.
[99] Waltke, 1.III.

expected or even promised,[100] but that God is at times even the One who causes calamity[101] and authors suffering. "Often we learn as Christians only through suffering what we could not otherwise have gained without the pain endured."[102]

3. **Expression of trust in God (v 5):** This is the turning point of David's lament. It shows a change of mood that illustrates David's trust in God's existence, power, steadfast love, and faithfulness.[103] Having spoken truth of his suffering and alienation, he now speaks truth of his trust in God, based not on blind faith, but on "God's unfailing love and past provision... that God will see and help the one who cries out for help."[104]

4. **Vow to praise God (v 6):** Having cried out, addressing and petitioning the Lord in his suffering, David has made his complaint and requested help, and he has put his trust in God. He now vows to praise God,[105] "I will sing to the LORD, because he has dealt bountifully with me." Nothing has changed in David's circumstances since he began this lament. He is under the same attack as he sings verse 6 as he was in verse 1. Yet there is a change that does not seem to flow smoothly with the rest of the prayer, a declaration that the Sovereign God who has led David into an experience of abandonment, isolation, sorrow, and fear, has "dealt bountifully" with him. David's circumstances have not changed. What has changed is the transformation of his heart as he sings this lament, "biblical praise in a minor key."[106]

This transformation happens through what Bruckner describes as a "basic three-fold movement of growth" as the lamenter moves

---

[100] John 16:33
[101] Isaiah 45:7
[102] Waltke, 1.V.D. (commenting on Romans 5:1-5).
[103] Rojerson and McKay, 59.
[104] Bruckner, 184.
[105] *Ibid*.
[106] *Ibid,* 184.

from the initial isolation and distress, through "a decision to turn toward life, light, and God," and finally into a reconciliation and restoration of relationship as "a witness to the wonder and vulnerability of life."[107]

Conclusion

In the midst of adversity, biblical lament:

- Reminds us of God's presence and power
- Draws us into conversation with God
- Presents our complaints to the only One able to address them
- Reinforces our trust in God
- Helps us to praise God from the depths

Discussion

1. Write a short prayer that includes the elements of lament and pray it out loud (on your own or with someone else). What part was the easiest, most difficult, and most meaningful to write and to pray?
2. Read Psalm 77 at least twice. Can you see the elements of Biblical lament in it?

Devotion

PSALM 5: TO THE CHOIRMASTER: FOR THE FLUTES. A PSALM OF DAVID.

Give ear to my words, O LORD;
consider my groaning.
Give attention to the sound of my cry,
my King and my God,
for to you do I pray.
O LORD, in the morning you hear my voice;

---

[107] *Ibid*, 186.

*in the morning I prepare a sacrifice for you
and watch.*

*For you are not a God who delights in
wickedness;
evil may not dwell with you.
The boastful shall not stand before your eyes;
you hate all evildoers.
You destroy those who speak lies;
the* LORD *abhors the bloodthirsty and deceitful
man.*

*But I, through the abundance of your
steadfast love,
will enter your house.
I will bow down toward your holy temple
in the fear of you.
Lead me, O* LORD, *in your righteousness
because of my enemies;
make your way straight before me.*

*For there is no truth in their mouth;
their inmost self is destruction;
their throat is an open grave;
they flatter with their tongue.
Make them bear their guilt, O God;
let them fall by their own counsels;
because of the abundance of their
transgressions cast them out,
for they have rebelled against you.*

*But let all who take refuge in you rejoice;
let them ever sing for joy,
and spread your protection over them,*

*that those who love your name may exult in
you.
For you bless the righteous, O LORD;
you cover him with favor as with a shield.*

PART 2: DISCIPLING INTO SUFFERING

Called Alongside

> *The eye cannot say to the hand, "I have no need of you," nor again the head to the feet, "I have no need of you." On the contrary, the parts of the body that seem to be weaker are indispensable, and on those parts of the body that we think less honorable we bestow the greater honor, and our unpresentable parts are treated with greater modesty, which our more presentable parts do not require. But God has so composed the body, giving greater honor to the part that lacked it, that there may be no division in the body, but that the members may have the same care for one another. If one member suffers, all suffer together; if one member is honored, all rejoice together.*
> *– 1st Corinthians 12:21-26*

We are all members of the same body, and so when one member suffers, we all suffer. We are called to suffer alongside one another. This is a blessing, not a curse, and it starts by going to those who suffer.

At 5:47am on August 13, 2013, my dear friends Ron and Kathleen Duncan heard a knock at the door and saw a police car outside their window. Officer Wiggins knew the Duncan family and volunteered to perform one of the most difficult things we ask our police officers to do. In the short conversation that followed, Ron and Kathleen learned that their 20-year-old son Andrew had been killed along with five other young people in an automobile crash. They collapsed. Their son was dead.[108]

The person you are called to disciple is a sufferer, and you are called to share in that suffering. In the next chapters, we will look at discipling a person who is suffering. While our own suffering is of course difficult for us, it can be even more difficult to be in the presence of the suffering of others. We don't know what to do or what to say (or what not to say). We don't know how to help. We are perplexed with other questions we cannot answer, such as "why did this happen?", "why did it happen to them?", and "why did it not happen to me?" Along with our own sympathetic and empathetic grief, which is the image of God shining forth, we may have other feelings and attitudes that betray the flesh that still fights to suppress that image, including unrighteous anger, bitterness, and even self-righteousness. It is uncomfortable to go, listen, empathize, speak, and stay.

Yet we are called to do just that, because that is what Christ did, and He commanded us to follow Him.

Ron and Kathleen heard many other knocks on the door on that terrible day. People who loved them and who loved Andrew came to show them love. Nobody, even the pastor, knew what to do or what to say. Some people brought food. Others brought stories. Some brought comfort. Then in the afternoon there was another knock, one that Kathleen says was more impactful than any other since the one at 5:47am. It was a mutual friend of ours who came within an hour of learning of Andrew's death. "Jeff had clearly been crying. He came in, wrapped his arms around Ron and me and said, 'There are no words. I am sorry. I love you.' This is exactly what you should say to a grieving parent: **There are no words. I am sorry you are going through this. I love you.**"[109]

---

[108] Kathleen Duncan, *What Bereaved Parents Want You to Know (But May Not Say)*, (Wichita Falls, TX: R & K Publishing, 2015), 2.
[109] *Ibid*, 23.

We are called to make disciples, and our disciples will suffer. Do not wait to share in their suffering until you know what to say to share God's comfort. Often, there are no words at first. Praise be to God that we can start sharing His comfort by simply showing up.

Discussion

1. Why do you think Kathleen believes Jeff's visit was more impactful than those of others?
2. Who is someone who has had a great ministry to you in your suffering? What stands out about that person's ministry?

Devotion

PSALM 84 TO THE CHOIRMASTER: ACCORDING TO THE GITTITH. A PSALM OF THE SONS OF KORAH.

How lovely is your dwelling place,
O LORD of hosts!
My soul longs, yes, faints
for the courts of the LORD;
my heart and flesh sing for joy
to the living God.

Even the sparrow finds a home,
and the swallow a nest for herself,
where she may lay her young,
at your altars, O LORD of hosts,
my King and my God.
Blessed are those who dwell in your house,
ever singing your praise! Selah

Blessed are those whose strength is in you,
in whose heart are the highways to Zion.
As they go through the Valley of Baca
they make it a place of springs;

the early rain also covers it with pools.
They go from strength to strength;
each one appears before God in Zion.

O LORD God of hosts, hear my prayer;
give ear, O God of Jacob! Selah
Behold our shield, O God;
look on the face of your anointed!

For a day in your courts is better
than a thousand elsewhere.
I would rather be a doorkeeper in the house of
my God
than dwell in the tents of wickedness.
For the LORD God is a sun and shield;
the Lord bestows favor and honor.
No good thing does he withhold
from those who walk uprightly.
O LORD of hosts,
blessed is the one who trusts in you!

Showing up: The Ministry of Presence

The Power of Showing Up

The ministry of presence always precedes the ministry of intercession.[110] It is often difficult, but always necessary, to enter into suffering of others if we are to disciple them. Christ Himself, in His sovereignty and omnipotence, able to accomplish all things from a distance, ministered in person and was never hesitant to be in the presence of suffering. There is a particular power in presence that addresses a critical need in the life of sufferers: to know that they are not alone.

> *Now when Job's three friends heard of all this evil that had come upon him, they came each from his own place, Eliphaz the Temanite, Bildad the Shuhite, and Zophar the Naamathite. They made an appointment together to come to show him sympathy and comfort him. And when they saw him from a distance, they did not recognize him. And they raised their voices and wept, and they tore their robes and sprinkled dust on their heads toward heaven. And they sat with him on the ground seven days and seven nights, and no one spoke a word to him, for they saw that his suffering was very great.*
> *– Job 2:11-13*

In 1993, Martha and I were stationed in Grand Forks, North Dakota, where I was flying bomber aircraft. Though we hadn't been at all excited when we received the assignment, we had found it to be a wonderful place to live. The extremely harsh weather and

---

[110] Gary Moore, "Samuel: His Call, Service, and Rejection," Sermon, (Loudon, NH: Faith Community Bible Church, Jan 1, 2023).

remote location had helped foster close relationships with our squadron, our community, and our church. My brother Matt just graduated from the Naval Academy and had come out to visit.

Our crew was returning from a multi-hour training flight. Normally, we would spend the next hour or so doing "transition," practicing approaches and landings, before making the final landing. Today, the command post called us on the radio and requested that we make our first approach to a "full stop." There was no explanation, which wasn't abnormal. After parking and postflight, we walked into the squadron where I was told that Martha was OK, but that she had been admitted to the base hospital. I excused myself from the debriefing and headed over, concerned but not anxious.

Martha was pale and in a good bit of abdominal pain when I arrived. Matt told me he found her collapsed on the floor upstairs. The doctors were not sure what was wrong, only that she was experiencing "flu-like symptoms" and that they were awaiting the results of tests. In the meantime, Martha was receiving IV fluids to treat her dangerously severe dehydration.

A little while later, a nurse came in to tell us that they still did not know what was causing the sickness, but that a routine test indicated Martha was pregnant. We had been trying to conceive for some time, and this was great news. Martha and I hugged and kissed. Matt hugged and congratulated me. We were parents!

Shortly afterwards, a doctor arrived with much less joyous news. Martha had significant internal bleeding. Based on further blood tests and her symptoms, they suspected an ectopic pregnancy and likely a tubal rupture. Ultrasounds confirmed this diagnosis. The baby was dead. Martha's life was in danger. She would need emergency surgery to stop the bleeding. A transfusion was started, but Martha seemed to get even paler and weaker.

The room became a blur of activity. As Martha was prepared, the surgeon arrived to tell us what was involved. The surgery wasn't especially complex but given the amount of blood she had lost and the rate she was still losing it, the risks were high. In fact, had Matt not been visiting and found her when he did, she likely would already have been dead. He was going to do his best, but there was a chance that Martha might not survive. I had only a few moments to say goodbye to Martha and give her a kiss before she was wheeled away into surgery. Matt and I were in an empty room.

I don't remember how Father Mike Williams, the rector of Saint Paul's Episcopal Church where we were active members, found out that Martha was ill. I don't remember him arriving. I don't remember anything he said. I don't remember him reading Scripture or praying. I know he did all of these things, in part because I know that this is what godly people like Mike do, but I don't remember any specifics about them.

What I do remember is that he was there, and that he stayed with me until Martha returned from surgery. And just the act of showing up had great power, a power I still can't really explain or understand but can still remember. For those horrible hours, Mike was Jesus to me.

Some time later, I asked Mike what he had done to make such a difference that day. What had he said? He told me he had said very little, and that beyond telling him what was happening with Martha, I had said very little as well. I insisted that he must have done something – because his being there changed things. I am not saying that it changed the outcome of Martha's surgery, or that it somehow lessened my sorrow. But it certainly changed my experience. In the depths of my despair, I know I experienced Christ's comfort, and I wanted to know what he had done to help that happen.

Mike answered that the only thing he had done was practice what he called the "ministry of presence." There is, he said, a particular power to simply showing up in the name of Jesus. It was what Jesus Himself often did in the presence of pain – he went to the sufferer and was present in the suffering. Throughout the gospels, we read how Jesus travelled to and waded into sickness, spiritual oppression, sin, sorrow, and death.[111] Of course, the most amazing example of Jesus' practice of the ministry of presence was in His coming into the

---

[111] Ex: John 4: 1-26, 46-54; 11:1-44.

world to be Immanuel, God with us, to be with us in the worst kind of human suffering, our separation from our loving Father. By being with people in their suffering, Mike was imitating Jesus.

Over the next year, I began to take notice of how Mike and his wife Becky practiced this ministry, walking into the presence of hurt, loss, and grief. As we moved on to further assignments, I found myself called to walk into the presence of others' sufferings. I contacted Mike from time to time for advice about how to do this better. Sometime along the way I began to realize that the power of presence was not only in the immediate comfort people received, but in how Mike had, by practicing this ministry, taught me to do the same. Mike had called me to imitate him as he imitated Christ. This is discipleship.

The God of Presence

> *"Our hope is not found in understanding why God allowed suffering into our lives. Our hope is not found in the belief that somehow we will tough our way through. Our hope is not found in doctors, lawyers, pastors, family, or friends. Our hope is not found in our resilience or ingenuity. Our hope is not found in ideas or things. Though we may look to all those for temporary help, ultimately our hope rests in the faithful and gracious presence of the Lord with us."*
> *– Paul Tripp*[112]

The triune God of the Bible stands apart from the gods worshipped by other religions because of His presence. From the beginning, God reveals Himself as one of relationship. He creates mankind in His own image, and then blesses, speaks to, cares and

---

[112] Tripp, 147.

provides for them.[113] God creates them as His representative to the rest of creation, filled with His breath, and entrusted with His work.[114] After creating everything in the world and calling it good, though, He finds one aspect of the first human's life not to be good – that he is alone. And so, He creates a companion, a help-meet, to hold fast to and become one flesh, so that they might be in relationship with one another,[115] better able to represent the God who Himself is one of relationship.

Even after those first humans spurn relationship with their Creator to seek their own self-rule, God reveals Himself further as the one who comes, who is present. When Moses asks for assurance, God replies "I will be with you."[116] Later God leads His commission to Moses' successor Joshua by promising His presence. "Just as I was with Moses, so I will be with you... Do not be frightened, and do not be dismayed, for the LORD your God is with you wherever you go."[117] His people repeat the sins of their forefathers, returning time and time again to that which does not bring life, God continues to promise His presence and then follow through with that promise. It is one of His most common assurances, and it becomes a blessing given by one person to another, "The LORD be with you."[118]

As mentioned earlier, the ultimate example of God's ministry of presence is displayed in God the Son coming into our world. Jesus, though being God Himself, emptied Himself, took on not just human form but that of a servant, humbling Himself even to death, so that we might be restored into relationship with Him.[119] It is the epitome of His display of love for us, to be so filled with that love as to be willing to meet us in our home, in our mess, in our fallen-ness. He desires to be with us, and He desires us to be with Him. In His darkest hour, Jesus Himself called His disciples to stay with Him, to

---

[113] Gen 1:26-31.
[114] Gen 2:7-15.
[115] Gen 2:18-25.
[116] Exo 3:12.
[117] Jsh 1:5-9.
[118] c.f. Rth 2:4; 1 Sa 17:37; 2 Sa 14:17; Amo 5:14.
[119] Phi 2:2-11.

be present with Him and watch over Him as He cried out to His Father.[120]

And then, having come to us, lived among us, taught us, and ultimately died for us, God was not willing to be apart from us in the time that lay between Jesus' resurrection and return. And so, He comes to us again, this time sending God the Holy Spirit, to dwell not just among but in us, fulfilling Jesus' promise to His disciples, "and behold, I am with you always, to the end of the age."[121]

Our Call to Presence

Through these and other examples, Jesus is calling us to imitate Him, to grow more like Him, including in how He enters into the suffering of others. This God, the God who in His perfect love is present, Immanuel, God with us, commands us to follow Him and to love one another just as He has loved us.[122] We act out and grow in our Christlikeness, loving others as we ourselves have been loved by Him, by being present with them, especially in their suffering. "When Christians express their care for another by being present," Sonny Guild writes, "they are also expressing Jesus' loving concern. We are more familiar with being his body. The Christian, a member of the community of faith, is a priest in the service of God. The priest brings the Father onto the scene. It may not be spoken. It may be a prayer. It may only be knowing and being thankful we share a relatedness because of God. Nevertheless, through our caring, we share the presence of the Father."[123]

Our call to be present is not a promise that this ministry will be easy. Over the course of my life, I developed what I think could accurately be described as a phobia of hospitals – not from my own experiences of illness or injury, but because of my experiences with loved ones suffering and dying. My heart would start pounding on

---

[120] Mk 14:32-42.
[121] Mt 28:20.
[122] Mk 8:34; Jn 13:34.
[123] Sonny Guild, "The Ministry of Presence: A Biblical View," *Leaven* (Pepperdine University), Volume 2, Issue 2, Jan 1, 1992.

the way to the hospital, and often I would be sweating as I entered the building. I could be irritable, nervous, and even physically shaking. This, by the way, was one of my biggest hesitations about entering vocational ministry. I feared that I would be called to visit hospitals more often. I also worried I would not be an effective minister of the gospel in those visits. I prayed and trusted that God would overcome this obstacle. He answered that prayer, but not in a way I perceived as gentle. Immediately after taking up my new role as associate pastor, our congregation and community entered a season of shockingly high incidences of sickness and death considering our modest size. I was visiting the Concord Hospital so often that many of the staff knew me by sight, and I began to refer to it jokingly as our "South Campus." I sat with people in waiting rooms, emergency departments, hospital rooms, intensive care units, and hospice houses. I will admit that at least at first, I went not because I wanted to but because I knew that I was called to do it. It was simply disciplined obedience. But then, at some point in those first few months, I realized I was not nearly as afraid of the hospital anymore. Looking back over the years since, I believe I have been delivered from this phobia to the point that I often look forward to the surprises of grace that God will display during visits.

I am not relaying this story to boast. I still have a severe dislike for, and a bit of fear of, hospitals, and this proves that I am still lacking in both thankfulness and faith. Nor am I telling you that if you but respond to God's call with obedience that He will remove all the barriers and difficulties that lay before you. But I do believe that God will give us what we need to be obedient to what He commands, and that He commanded each of us to be present in the suffering of others. Thus, He comforts "us in all our affliction, so that we may be able to comfort those who are any affliction, with the comfort with which we ourselves are comforted by God."[124]

---

[124] 2 Co 1:4.

If God has called you to be a disciple-maker, and He has, He will provide you with the comfort you need to comfort the person you are discipling. And this comfort will start with presence.

Preparing to Go

Preparation is important to the ministry of presence. Of course, the time available to prepare can vary from seconds to days, but as time and circumstances permit, we will be more effective at sharing in comforts and sufferings with the people we disciple if we spend time and effort preparing to go.

Prayer should be the first, last, and continuing aspect of any ministry, including the ministry of presence. Praying on behalf of the sufferer is important. Perhaps equally important is to pray for ourselves to be bold yet humble, quick to hear and slow to speak, patient and wise in our responses, and longsuffering in our endurance. In other words, we should pray that Jesus' nature would shine through us. The opening line of the prayer often attributed to Francis of Assisi might be a good start. In fact, in a situation that affords little time to prepare, it might suffice. "Lord, let me be an instrument of your love."

Consider asking others who will be faithful to also pray for you as you go. Be mindful here of the discipline of discretion. While it may be appropriate to give many details about the suffering into which you are going, it may be sufficient to tell your friends that you are going to visit a person in distress, asking them to pray for that unnamed person and that you would be Christlike in your actions, words, and attitudes.

Preparation should also include physical practicalities. Silencing your mobile phone, or perhaps leaving it in your car, may be the first of such preparations. Having your Bible on hand is always a good idea, and to that I add a notebook, pen, and often a hymnal. If time permits, you might change into clothes that are comfortable, presentable, and appropriate for the context. I like to dress in layers as I find hospitals, for instance, to be quite cold, while some people tend to run the heat up quite high in their houses. I never regret having a pocket-sized pack of tissues on hand. Think what might be helpful or appreciated: a cup of coffee, a spray of flowers, a plate of baked goods, or a meal. Knowing the person and environment you are visiting, you may make other preparations, but at the forefront of your mind should be the fact that the most important thing you are brining is your presence, and specifically your presence as an image-bearer, a minister of God.

Mental preparation is likewise vital. Pray that God will give you insight into your weaknesses, fears, aversions, and proclivities. He may provide that answer through someone who knows you well and will give you straight and honest answers. Ask God to walk you through those difficulties and to strengthen your faith in Him – it is in His nature to do so![125]

Sometimes the notice for entering into suffering affords us a long time to prepare, such as supporting an old friend in another town at the funeral of a loved one. There are many opportunities to pray and prepare as you make your reservations, pack, and travel. Make wise use of this gift of time!

At other times there seems to be no time at all. Perhaps you meet a person you are discipling and ask him how the past week went. He answers that it has gone well, but you can see he is holding something back. There is a shakiness to his voice, perhaps a watering and aversion of his eyes. What you do next may determine whether he lets you enter into his suffering or brushes it aside, shutting you out. You may only have time for a quick and silent appeal to God for help. Make that plea and step out in faith, not in your own strength, but in the One who strengthens you! A wonderful two-verse prayer to memorize for these times might be:

I lift my eyes to the hills.
From where does my help come?

---

[125] Ps 21:4; Mk 9:23-25.

> *My help comes from the LORD,*
> *who made heaven and earth.*
> *– Psalm 121:1-2*

An even shorter prayer is the plea a woman made to Jesus on behalf of her son: "Lord, help me!"[126]

Remember also that though we do not know what tomorrow will hold, we have at least this moment. We can start our preparations now, praying God helps us prepare for the next time we are called to enter into suffering.

Entering into Suffering

The first step of any journey is often the hardest. This seems particularly so when our journey takes us into the presence of suffering. Our hesitations stem from a mix of godly and ungodly motives, and it is frequently difficult to discern between the two. I might tell myself I do not want to impose, I want to allow the person "space," or I would only get in the way. This all may spring from godly desires not to cause more discomfort or suffering to a hurting person, or from a selfish desire not to be uncomfortable myself. I may tell myself I don't know what to say, how to help, or what to do. This might flow from godly humility, or the pride of thinking I am the one responsible for providing the words, help, or actions.

Let us then simplify the choice of action. If God placed a person in your life to disciple, He has called you to enter into that person's suffering. Doing so may be uncomfortable for both of you. There may be times when you make mistakes, maybe terrible mistakes, and add to the suffering rather than provide comfort. There may be long, awkward times where you don't know what to say or do; seven days and nights would not be unprecedented.[127] Despite all of this, go. Go. Be present.

---

[126] Mt 15:27.
[127] Job 2:13.

> "Most people do not ask for help. Even desperate people are slow to ask for help. So we take the initiative and move toward each other. God has moved towards us; we move toward others in his name... And if we feel a little awkward? All the better... We move toward others, not because we can do these things with ease but because of Jesus."
> – Ed Welch[128]

Don't wait to be asked. Don't wait to be ready. Don't wait to be able. Go because of your Father's will, go because you are following Jesus, go because you are empowered by the Spirit.

Use godly prudence, of course. Pray before you go. Be considerate regarding time and location.[129] But go. Make an appointment if appropriate and be gentle yet persistent about it. Step up to the door, continue in prayer, and then knock. If there is no answer, leave a note and come again later. Show up where the sufferer waits, whether it is the hospital, hospice house, church building, funeral home, or courtroom. If you absolutely cannot be there, then of course call, write, text, or email. But when you are able, go. There is no substitute for the physical presence of an image-bearer of the God of presence, a representative follower of Jesus Christ the sufferer, a person indwelled by the Spirit called παράκλητος, the Helper, Advocate, and Comforter.[130]

In times of deep suffering, your greeting need not be wordy at all. Remember my friend Jeff's words to Ron and Kathleen soon after the death of their son. "There are no words. I'm sorry. I love you."

---

[128] Edward T. Welch, *Side by Side: Walking with Others in Wisdom and Love*, (Wheaton, IL: Crossway, 2015), 73, 76.
[129] Pro 27:14.
[130] Jn 14:26.

Sitting in the Ashes

Shortly after I began working as a vocational pastor, Todd, a member of our congregation who struggled with cancer for many years, began a precipitous decline. Within weeks he was in Concord Hospital's hospice house, and our Senior Pastor invited me to accompany him on a visit. It was my first time in that facility but certainly not my last. Once we passed the locked doors and sign-in desk, we were greeted by a quiet, friendly, clean, comfortable, and welcoming space. But stepping into Todd's room was like stepping from an outer courtyard into a temple or sanctuary. The curtains were drawn, and the lights were low. Greetings were spoken in hushed tones. We sat in silence, weeping, as Todd pleaded with God to take him home and his wife Sue pleaded with God to heal him so that he could stay. Later, one of the nurses – not a believer to my knowledge – told me that walking into Todd's room made her feel like she was entering into a "holy place."

Do you remember the last time you entered what felt like a holy place? Maybe it was a cathedral or other house of worship, or perhaps a cemetery. Did you find yourself responding initially with silence?

Recently our family was in the mountains of Switzerland in an area said to be the inspiration for Tolkien's mythical land of Rivendell. One of our hikes was into the Chilchbalm valley. At the end of the trail, the forest seemed to part suddenly, and we found ourselves in a vast wildflower-filled arena surrounded by steep mountains. A river was flowing out of a glacier, and no less than seventeen waterfalls poured out of the cliffs above. God's display of His awesome creative power made us feel not just small but miniscule and insignificant. It was a holy place. We were struck mute.

When we enter into holiness, silence is usually our natural response. When we enter into the suffering of another, we are "stepping into a holy place, into the other person's unique universe of selfhood, need, and pain. It is holy because when you enter, you will find Jesus already there ahead of you, in that unique person.

What a privilege!"[131] After the initial greetings, the expressions of compassion, our silence may be the appropriate next response. We may reach out with a gentle touch, depending on our relationship and the sufferer's comfort: a handshake, a hand on the shoulder, a hug. But it is our silence, not our words, which should characterize our presence in such a holy place.

Job's friends are much maligned for their unwise and hurtful words. But we must remember that they started off as an example of loving and caring support. They heard of Job's suffering, travelled great distances, sympathized with him, and then lovingly and respectfully sat in the ashes with him in silence for a full week.[132]

Silence is an uncomfortable void we seek to fill. Most of us cannot leave the driveway without some sort of information pouring into our ears, be it phone, radio, podcast, music, or video reels. And even as we absorb these inputs (often multiple sources at once), we also participate in a near-constant stream of output by speaking, texting, and videoing. It appears we will do just about anything to avoid the discomfort of silence. "One reason we can hardly bear to remain silent," Richard Foster writes, "is that it makes us feel so helpless. We are so accustomed to relying on words to manage and control others... The tongue is our most powerful weapon of manipulation... Silence is one of the deepest Disciplines of the Spirit simply because it puts the stopper on that."[133]

The ministry of presence relies upon the discipline of silence. We are an easily distracted people. In this age of constant access to a plethora of information and media (and access to us), it is particularly easy for us to be proximate yet not present. Entering into the suffering of others requires that we leave those distractions

---

[131] Kenneth Haugk, *Don't Sing Songs to a Heavy Heart: How to Relate to Those Who Are Suffering*, (St Louis, MO: Stephen Ministries, 2004), 35.
[132] Job 2:11-13.
[133] Richard J. Foster, *Celebration of Discipline: The Path to Spiritual Growth*, (San Francisco, CA: Harper & Row, 1978), 88.

behind to focus on who and what God put before us. Foster continues:

> *One of the fruits of silence is the freedom to let our justification rest entirely with God. We don't need to straighten others out. There is a story of a medieval monk who was being unjustly accused of certain offenses. One day he looked out his window and watched a dog biting and tearing on a rug that had been hung out to dry. As he watched, the Lord spoke to him saying, 'That is what I am doing to your reputation. But if you will trust Me you will not need to worry about the opinions of others.' Perhaps more than anything else, silence brings us to believe that God can justify and set things straight...*[134]

> *...The tongue is a thermometer; it tells us our spiritual temperature. It is also a thermostat; it controls our spiritual temperature. Control of the tongue can mean everything. Have we been set free so that we can hold our tongue? Bonhoeffer wrote, 'Real silence, real stillness, real spiritual stillness.' Dominic is reported to have visited Francis of Assisi and throughout the entire meeting neither spoke a single word. Only when we have learned to be truly silent are we enabled*

---

[134] Ibid.

> *to speak the word that is needed when it is needed.* [135]

Silence enables us to look and listen rather than think and speak. Much like first responders are trained to approach any scene both focusing on the details and taking in the broader picture, we can begin to take in the scene into which God has brought us. We can focus on the sufferer: her demeanor, words, manner, and appearance. We can take in the environment: sights, sounds, smells, feelings, and others who might be present.

Most importantly, we can pray silently, opening the ears and eyes of our hearts to God and expressing ourselves to Him. During these initial times of silence, when we know very little of what specifically is happening, we can pray very simply, trusting that God knows what is needed before we even ask.[136] Our prayer may be as simple as "Lord, have mercy." We come to show sympathy and provide comfort. We start by sitting in silence, for we see that the suffering is very great. This is discipleship.

Discussion

1. Can you remember a time of suffering when a person's presence was so powerful that you would consider it a manifestation of Jesus' presence?
2. What commonly holds you back from being present in the suffering of another?

Devotion

> *Two are better than one, because they have a good reward for their toil. For if they fall, one will lift up his fellow. But woe to him who is alone when he falls and has not another to lift him up! Again, if two lie together, they keep warm, but how can one keep warm*

---

[135] *Ibid*, 88-89.
[136] Mt 6:8.

alone? And though a man might prevail against one who is alone, two will withstand him—a threefold cord is not quickly broken.
– Ecclesiastes 4:9-12

Inclining Our Ears: The Ministry of Listening

Quick to Hear

Having entered into the presence of suffering, the next task is to listen. In our discomfort with suffering, we often try to soften, minimize, silence, or otherwise answer the cries of the sufferer. Yet Scripture teaches us, "if one gives an answer before he hears, it is his folly and shame."[137] Responding to suffering requires that we first hear it. In this chapter, we will consider some of the principles, techniques, and barriers to listening not simply effectively, but compassionately. Our primary purpose in listening is not simply to gain information so that we might be able to comprehend and begin fixing the problem. Listening is first a ministry to the sufferer through allowing the person to share his or her experiences of suffering.

Listening to the One Who Suffers Expressively

In the cultures in which the Bible was written, grief often was shared and even public, expressive, and visible. "Mourning included visible rites such as loud weeping and wailing, tearing clothes, self-mutilation, shaving the head and beard, fasting, and placing dirt on the head." [138] Even poorer families were expected to employ professional mourners after the death of loved ones. These expressions of grief are foreign to Western culture. Our English translations of Scripture have difficulty even conveying the emotions Jesus felt as He approached Lazarus' tomb. The ESV presents Jesus as "deeply moved in his spirit and greatly troubled,"[139] a translation D.A. Carson bristles at. "Most English translations soften the passage to 'He groaned in spirit', 'He sighed heavily', 'He was deeply touched' or, as here, 'He was deeply moved in spirit'—all without

---

[137] Pro 18:13.
[138] Mark J. Boda and Gordon J. McConville, Eds., *Dictionary of the Old Testament: Prophets*, (Downers Grove, IL: IVP Academic, 2012), 473.
[139] Jn 11:33.

linguistic justification."[140] John then writes, "Jesus wept."[141] He wept openly, observably, and unashamedly.

While we should lean towards silence, there is no reason to quiet the sufferer. Strangely, we tend to be uncomfortable both with the weight of silence and with emotional expressions of grief. We often have a visceral urge to silence, or at least mitigate cries. "There, there... It will be OK" feels like a comforting thing to say because it offers *us* hope that these cries of pain can be hushed and *our* discomfort eased. But muting or minimizing the cries of sufferers adds nothing to their comfort. On the contrary, these words can be caustic and hurtful. Instead, we should seek to help the sufferer give voice to his or her pain. "Sometimes," writes Kenneth Haugk (founder of Stephen Ministries), "people just need to cry. Tears are cleansing. Denying tears can prevent them from working through and cleaning out their pain right at the most appropriate and beneficial time for this cleansing."[142] In fact, those tears often can be a window that helps us see beyond the immediate or obvious cause of suffering and into the background and nuance of the sufferer's experience. I learned a helpful question in this vein from Ed Welch: "If your tears could speak, what would they say?"

And then, as the sufferer speaks, we listen.

Listening to the One Who Suffers in Silence

At other times, the tears don't flow at all. Many times, this is because the sufferer has been taught to endure suffering with false Stoicism, denying or at least suppressing grief. Consider how many times we have told ourselves the lie "it's not worth crying about" when it certainly was. How many times, in your childhood or adulthood, did you recite rhymes like "Sticks and stones may break

---

[140] D.A. Carson, *The Gospel according to John: The Pillar New Testament Commentary*, (Grand Rapids, MI: Inter-Varsity Press; W.B. Eerdmans, 1991), 495.
[141] Jn 11:35.
[142] (Haugk 2004, 66).

my bones, but words can never hurt me"? Yet deep down you know, and Scripture agrees with you, that words do hurt.[143]

We should invite and encourage people to speak words to the suffering, but we should not compel them to do so. It may be that there are no words yet to express the pain or sorrow. The sufferer may not feel safe to speak to you in the existing environment, or in the present company. Shame is also a powerful deterrent to speaking, and it is not necessarily shame for one's own failings. Sometimes, I found those who have been abused or betrayed, particularly by spouses, to be extremely reluctant to reveal their abuser's or betrayer's sin because of the immense and complex shame that afflicts victims of those particular sins.

In these times, we assure the sufferer that we are willing to sit beside him or her in that silence. And then we sit. While some are better gifted than others with abiding in discomfort as silence hangs heavy in the room, most of us have to learn the discipline of doing so. I have found it helpful to pray silently for the sufferer, for others involved, and for God to use me. The three verses of Psalm 131 compose a passage upon which I have found helpful to memorize and meditate in such times:

PSALM 131: A SONG OF ASCENTS. OF DAVID.

O Lord, my heart is not lifted up;
my eyes are not raised too high;

I did not occupy myself with things
too great and too marvelous for me.

But I have calmed and quieted my soul,
like a weaned child with its mother;
like a weaned child is my soul within me.

---

[143] Pro 12:15; 18:21.

> *O Israel, hope in the Lord*
> *from this time forth and forevermore.*

Remain focused on the sufferer and resist the urge to break the silence or avoid it through distractions or busyness. Smartphones, agendas, daydreams, fidgeting, and side conversations will all offer to rescue us from our discomfort. Fetching a cup of water or coffee can be an act of care. Excusing oneself to the restroom may be a necessity. Repetitive errands of this nature convey impatience and fatigue, which sufferers are likely to perceive, perhaps correctly, as meaning we are impatient with or fatigued by them.

I practice two exceptions to this principle of silence: Scripture and spoken prayers. In a time of extended silence, I ask the sufferer, "Would it be OK if I read a passage from Scripture?" or, "Would you mind if I prayed?" Which comes first depends on the circumstances, but usually I do both. In either case, I lean towards brevity, and allow silence to continue between and afterwards so that the Scripture and prayer can speak into the grief rather than become tools to escape it. In the Appendix, I offer suggested passages for various circumstances.

As the silence continues, we continue to listen in it.

Listening to a Sufferers' Story

When the silence breaks or the sobbing subsides and the sufferer starts speaking, let that telling continue! While barriers as discussed above might keep the sufferer from speaking, "hurting people usually want to talk about their life situations. They will seize the opportunity to do so when given a chance. Your immediate goal is simply getting them to talk about what is concerning them right at that moment. That will be enough, if you allow it to happen. You don't have to think up the perfect formula answers to questions. You don't have to theologize or psychologize or sing away the other's heavy heart. You probably couldn't do it anyway."[144] We are here for the long haul, to help the sufferer walk through this valley. We

---

[144] Haugk, 55.

start by resisting the urge to fill in details, share similar stories, or give advice, and simply letting the sufferer tell his or her story.

As the story unfolds, we listen, clarify when necessary, and repeat to make sure we have heard correctly.

And we continue to pray. We pray not necessarily for a "fix," but instead that our hearts be softened, our ears opened, our patience expanded, and, when the time does come to speak, that our words will be gentle and compassionate. Again, Haugk offers a helpful framework for how we can listen and let the sufferer unfold his or her grief:

> Follow the other person's lead, focus on them, and be careful with sharing our own experiences.[145]

1. **Follow the other person's lead**: Rather than adding your insights, express sorrow while listening to understand the sufferer's mind and heart. Typically, people who are grieving or in pain have conflicting feelings. Their thoughts may shift back and forth rapidly. Let them take the lead, and thus show you value and prize them. This is an act of humility, acknowledging your limited understanding.[146]
2. **Focus on the other person**: "Remember from the beginning that your conversation with a suffering person is not about "us" – meaning not about you *and* the other person, as conversations usually flow. It is strictly about the one who is suffering. This conversation is between unequals because, at that moment, one person has a heavier load to carry than the other." This is how we express unconditional love like in the same manner as Jesus. We are coming to serve rather than to be served.[147] Unless you are expressing sorrow and compassion, be alert to how often you are using first person pronouns like "I," "me," and "my."

---

[145] *Ibid*, 56-58.
[146] *Ibid*, 57.
[147] Mk 10:45.

3. **Be careful when sharing personal experiences**: There are times to share personal experiences — perhaps to express your empathy — but be sparing in doing so. It is better to err towards sharing later rather than earlier. If you do choose to share, do so briefly, and consider how your experience and the manner in which you convey it could harm rather than help.[148]

Disciplined Listening

Even before 2020, when "virtual meeting" became a common term in the general public, many of us were familiar with various video-calling services. Since then, "virtual" is a near-omnipresent modifier to all manner of human interaction. We speak of "virtual learning," "virtual medicine," "virtual assistant," "virtual counseling," "virtual baby shower," "virtual date," "virtual friend," and even a term that still causes me to bristle: "virtual church."

My irritation is one of preference and principle rather than core Gospel doctrine, but it does speak to my ecclesiology (beliefs about the Church). I believe the Church is called to gather together to worship, that this worship is meant to be communication rather than performance, and that communication is a two-way street. Though some of our community's congregations succeeded in making livestreamed services interactive, the format nonetheless lends itself to passive watching rather than participation.

Listening is a discipline, an active endeavor that is so much more than the physiological sense of hearing. When walking in the woods, I might hear a twig break and then listen to determine its direction, source, and nature. Listening requires not only our ears, but our hearts and minds, bodies, other senses, and even our voices. It is a discipline that, like any other discipline, begins with preparation and is honed through practice.

---

[148] Haugk, 59-61.

Disciplined Listening Begins with Listening to God

While it is of course important to listen to the sufferer, disciplined listening begins with listening to God. "To understand man," writes former U.S. Army Chaplain Mike Stingley, "one must begin with the knowledge of God."[149] Said knowledge of God must start with the revelation about Himself that He provided in Scripture. This is yet another reason that anyone who would follow Jesus and obey His command to make disciples must be an ardent student of His Word. Our preparation to exegete (draw meaning out of) from a sufferer's words must start with exegeting God's Word. Only His Word provides us the foundational truths through which we can comprehend human suffering. This is a process that is quite difficult to start in the moment of need, when a sufferer is pouring out his heart to us. We must prepare ourselves beforehand with God's Word if we are to truly listen to the sufferer's cries.

Disciplined listening to God also requires us to avail ourselves of prayer, asking God to open not only <u>all</u> of our senses, but also our hearts. We ask God to incline our souls to Him so that we might not merely know about Him, but truly know Him. Jesus says that this knowledge of God is eternal life.[150] We also must ask God to open our senses and heart, and to incline our souls, toward the sufferer, that we might see clearly not only into the circumstances, but into the sufferer.

Disciplined Listening Involves More than the Ears

Our nonverbal cues communicate more powerfully than our actual words. Intentionally and/or unintentionally, we transmit messages via our facial expression, posture, gestures, breathing, the positioning of our legs and arms, and even where we choose to sit or stand. Others inevitably interpret such messages in ways that may or may not be correct.

---

[149] Mike Stingley, "Disciplined Listening," *The Journal of Biblical Counseling*, 1977: 52-56.
[150] Jn 17:3.

There are many resources for learning the intricacies of nonverbal communication, but some basic principles include positioning ourselves to face and lean towards the other person with an open posture. Specifically, legs and arms should be uncrossed, hands open or loosely interlaced rather than clenched or closed, eyes should look at rather than avoid the other person. An active listener should acknowledge with nods, shoulder and hand movements, sighs, and murmurs. We should be intentional about what we are conveying but need not force or "fake" it. If you think about it, much of this likely comes somewhat naturally. Consider how your posture changes instinctively when a child comes to you with a skinned knee. You turn toward her, crouch down, lean in, look into her eyes and at her injury, and engage with movement and touch. Your eyes and face even "soften" – something we have difficulty describing yet know when we see it happen.

I found writing to be another extremely powerful tool for good listening. Several years ago, I realized that my attempts at journaling on a computer inevitably resulted in me being distracted by the myriad other opportunities on that device. Instead, I began carrying a bound notebook along with my Bible, and I started writing my reflections in it along with notes from Bible studies, devotions, sermons, prayer requests, and pastoral care visits. Quite by accident, I discovered that taking notes on my phone or tablet while people were speaking distracted them or caused them to think I was distracted. Conversely, taking written notes conveyed that I was listening more closely and even assured them that I would indeed follow up in prayer and otherwise.

Disciplined listening also requires observing nonverbal cues from the sufferer. We certainly listen to words and their tone, but also watch the sufferer's posture, gestures, and expressions. We notice cues like flushing, tensing, fidgeting, crying, sniffling, and shivering. We see when the eyes soften, harden, drop, focus, glaze, or divert. We hear changes in breathing. We feel the stiffness or softness of a touch or embrace. We observe when a sufferer keeps glancing at a photo on the wall. All these cues and more distinguish listening from mere hearing.

Disciplined Listening Involves our Voices

To listen effectively, we should also enlist the help of our voices. It may be counterintuitive to think that speaking will help us listen better. We should certainly lead with silence, being "quick to hear, slow to speak."[151] But imagine (or more likely, remember) speaking to someone who remained silent, asking no questions and not responding with as much as a grunt or "hmmm." A wall listens similarly.

Our voices should not interrupt the person's story, but just as turning or leaning away from the speaker indicates a lack of engagement, the absence of verbal interaction gives the sufferer valid reason to believe he or she is not being heard, and that the other person's attention is elsewhere. Such verbal absence creates distance rather than intimacy. We must interact appropriately with our voices if we are to listen well.

Again, we do this somewhat naturally. Returning to the injured child, as we crouch down, lean in, and listen to her cries, we add short questions, acknowledgements, and expressions of empathy. These cues allow her to tell her story and help us to comprehend her suffering. The same principles apply to listening to other stories of hurt. We speak not only with our words, but with our very breath. Consider how much can be communicated with only the depth and speed of our breath. A quick, short gasp might convey surprise, while a deeper, slower inhalation can indicate a deeper apprehension. Likewise, a sharp breath out between our teeth or pursed lips can show agitation, while an extended exhalation, particularly with drooping shoulders and lowered eyes, can communicate fatigue or sorrow.

Disciplined Listening Seeks to Hear

In the process of learning and practicing this discipline we must not forget we are listening with a purpose. We are listening to hear,

---

[151] Jas 1:19.

seeking to learn and understand the sufferer's experience and theology of suffering.

Hearing the Experience of Suffering

Our purpose is not to discern the facts and circumstances of what has happened. That is the work of fixing. Our purpose in these first conversations is to let the person share his or her experiences of suffering. There may in fact be a wide gulf between the objective truth of what has happened or is happening, and the suffering that a person has experienced and is experiencing. The objective fact that a monster is not living under a child's bed does not mean she is not suffering from fear, nor does it mean that the real source of her fear is that imagined monster. By careful listening her parent begins to understand the little girl's suffering, but more importantly, ministers to her by allowing her to voice that suffering.

We all have monsters. We all have fears. We all suffer. We need people to listen.

As we listen to the sufferer's story unfold, we may hear the facts and circumstances related to the suffering: death, broken bones or growing tumors, domestic abuse, estranged loved ones, financial loss, struggle with addiction, rejection, homelessness, or other events that have happened or are happening. These details and facts are important, and we need to hear them because these details may be crucial to lasting relief from this suffering, but *in the moment*, it is more important to the sufferer how he or she is experiencing those events.

In the relaying of those events, we hear the elements of perception and experience. How does the person see, hear, and feel these events physically, mentally, emotionally, and spiritually?

Earlier, I wrote of fracturing my back and ribs by falling off a horse. The doctor who treated me in the emergency room inquired what had happened and where I felt pain. She examined me and began making a plan for tests to determine the specifics of my injuries. She asked questions to learn the events and conditions that were causing my suffering. She then said she was going to give me morphine to help with the significant physical pain I was experiencing. I began to cry.

It would have been easy for the doctor to assume this was a reaction to the pain, or perhaps interpret it as tears of relief at the prospect of relief. Instead, she practiced disciplined listening and asked questions – in effect she asked what my tears were saying. In the short sentences I could manage in my pain, explained that as both a police officer and a pastor, I had seen the effects of opioids and they scared me much more than physical pain. By asking questions, this doctor learned not only facts and circumstances, but also how I was experiencing suffering in my particular context and frame of reference.

This is what we seek to do as we listen to a sufferer. We want to know what events are involved in the suffering, but beyond that, what is the sufferer telling us about how he or she is perceiving those events. What fears, sorrows, regrets, hopes, despairs, angers, irritations, loves, hates, desires, needs, past experiences, and other emotions or contexts are affecting his or her experience of suffering?

Hearing the Theology of Suffering

How the person perceives and experiences his or her suffering helps us to hear not only the experience of suffering, but also the person's theology of suffering. How does the suffering affect the sufferer's understanding of God, and how does the sufferer's understanding of God affect the experience of suffering? Sufferers may emphasize, de-emphasize, or even deny God's compassion or sovereignty. The sufferer may speak outright heresy. They may question God's presence, His care, His kindness, His power, or even His existence. These words may come from what the sufferer truly believes or be a result of the confusion and distortion of beliefs that often occurs with severe distress.

We listen with discipline, engaging our senses, asking questions, and above all, relying upon God for guidance and wisdom. What does the person fear, love, hate, value, regret, desire, need, or trust? In where, what, or whom does the person find safety, security, pleasure, value, or identity? What does the person believe about this suffering, its causes, its meanings, or its purposes?[152] We may explicitly ask these questions, or we may perceive the answers as we listen to the sufferer's story. The answers to these questions tell us the sufferer's theology of suffering, and you may see where this theology is missing the mark. But tread lightly. Again, at this point we are focusing on listening rather than teaching, rebuking, or correcting. When the time to speak does arrive, we should seek compassion and understanding before we seek remedies, for it is when our hearts align in this grief that we can best help the sufferer to bring his or her cries to God in lament.

Discussion

1. What have you learned over the course of your life about the proper way to express (or not express) suffering? How does that help or hinder your listening?
2. Is there a person you feel is very good at listening to the cries of suffering? What could you learn from him or her?

Devotion

PSALM 130: A SONG OF ASCENTS.

Out of the depths I cry to you, O LORD!
O LORD, hear my voice!
Let your ears be attentive
to the voice of my pleas for mercy!

If you, O LORD, should mark iniquities,
O LORD, who could stand?
But with you there is forgiveness,
that you may be feared.

---

[152] An excellent resource for a list of these and many more questions: David Powlison, "X-Ray Questions: Drawing out the Whys and Wherefores of Human Behavior," *The Journal of Biblical Counseling*, 1999, 2-9.

I wait for the L<small>ORD</small>, *my soul waits,*
and in his word I hope;
my soul waits for the L<small>ORD</small>
more than watchmen for the morning,
more than watchmen for the morning.

O Israel, hope in the L<small>ORD</small>*!*
For with the L<small>ORD</small> *there is steadfast love,*
and with him is plentiful redemption.
And he will redeem Israel
from all his iniquities.

Sharing in Suffering: The Ministry of Empathy

Tears of a Friend

Scripture commands us to "rejoice with those who rejoice, weep with those who weep."[153] Discipleship requires relationship, and relationship with a sufferer requires that we not only witness and hear that person's pain, but that we feel it. The literal meaning of compassion is to suffer together. To have compassion is to have such a deep awareness of a person's suffering as to consider it our own. Sometimes, this comes easily, especially for people with whom we are very closely bound, or in specific forms of suffering we ourselves experienced. At other times, compassion is difficult. We may have difficulty understanding that suffering, or even harbor an aversion to it or its apparent causes. Nevertheless, we are commanded to clothe ourselves in compassion[154] and called to be transformed into the likeness of Christ, the God who not only describes Himself over and over in His Scripture as compassionate and merciful, but also demonstrated that compassion in His life on earth.[155] This compassion leads us not only to help guide the sufferer in biblical lament, but to join in that lament ourselves, crying out to the God who hears and acts.

"The pain we hear is rightly answered with a compassionate response. That means we love those who suffer to the point that we are affected by their hardships. In a sense, compassion is enjoyment's companion. We enjoy good things in someone and have compassion during the hard things."[156]

Empathy and Compassion

The story is not unfamiliar to many of us. A son, filled with passions and dreams and tired of the burdens his parents put on him, leaves home and dives into the world. Rejecting so many of the

---

[153] Rom 12:15.
[154] Col 3:12.
[155] Ex 33:19; Psa 116:5; Isa 49:13; Mt 9:36.
[156] Welch (2015), 102.

values his parents tried to instill, he lives large for a time but eventually falls into difficulty, then failure, then ruin. He is filled with shame and knows that he has spent every penny and burnt every bridge. In despair, he swallows the little pride he has left and returns home to ask for help.

This is perhaps one of the most difficult people with whom to sympathize. His suffering is largely his own doing. His parents are the wronged party. They have been gravely hurt by the son they loved, raised, supported, and cared for. Instead of displaying gratitude, he turned his back on them and everything they value. They owe him nothing.

Jesus told a similar story, a parable in which a son boldly demands his father give him what he thinks he is owed. The son then rejects his father and his values, and goes off to squander his wealth in reckless living and prostitutes. When he comes to ruin, he returns home with his hat in his hand. Yet while the son is still a far way off, his father sees him and, filled with compassion, runs to him, interrupting his son's confession to embrace, kiss, and restore him to sonship.[157]

In Jesus' parable, the compassionate father represents God. God's unchanging nature, revealed to Moses in Exodus 34 and repeated to others throughout history, is one of compassion,[158] showing mercy and favor, often when our sense of justice would respond with rejection and punishment. He sees us in our suffering. He knows us in our suffering. And somehow, the King of the universe makes our sufferings His own. His heart breaks, He runs to us, embraces us, kisses us, and restores us. He is the compassionate Father.

Weep with Those Who Weep

Don's arms were crossed as he sat in my office next to his wife, Alyssa. His shoulders were rigid. His face was flint. The two of

---

[157] Lk 15:11-32.
[158] Ex 34:6

them asked to meet with me to discuss struggles they were having with parenting and marriage, but it was obvious that Don did not want to be here. This was not going to be easy.

Don and Alyssa had been coming to our church for a short time, drawn to us by a sense of "ought to" rather than a true faith. Alyssa started to be discipled by a woman in the church and was growing in faith. Don, a computer test engineer, remained a skeptic. His wife had been trying to convince him to meet with someone, but he did not have time for religious nonsense or some pastor who thought he could fix everything. Alyssa finally convinced him to come to me by pointing out our shared Air Force backgrounds. He agreed only reluctantly, and it did not take much training in non-verbal communication to see that.

I really did not know Don and Alyssa beyond what I learned in short conversations before and after services, so I asked if they could tell me about themselves. They had been married several years, each bringing two children from a previous marriage and divorce. There were more similarities in their backgrounds, they said.

Alyssa's story was one of abandonment by her parents and then her first husband. Her account was filled with pain and suffering.

I said little as she spoke except to clarify or draw out the narrative more. Only a few minutes into it my eyes began to water, and soon tears were rolling down my cheeks. All I could say to her was that I could not even begin to comprehend how it must feel to go through what she had, and that I was sorry she had suffered so badly.

I was not the only one whose demeanor changed as Alyssa spoke. Don began to soften as well. His shoulders drooped. His arms uncrossed. His hands relaxed. His face became warm. I noted silently that his compassion for his wife was strong and real, and that this would be an asset in the future if I could continue meeting with them.

Don's story was next, and the parallels were stunning. His wife also abandoned him and their two young girls. I continued to weep as he spoke, and soon all three of us were doing our best to keep tissue manufacturers financially stable. Again, I had no words except to note the similarity of their suffering, the severity of it, and my grief at their pain.

I know I prayed during that meeting, both silently and aloud. I don't remember the specifics, but I am fairly certain it was a prayer of lament. That is my default in times of suffering. It is my comfort food.

Beyond that, I don't remember if I had any wise counsel for them. We agreed to meet again.

There is much more to their stories, but here is a supersonic flyby: Don and Alyssa both came to Christ. They didn't do it tentatively, either. I entered into a long-term discipling relationship with Don, and it was an exhilarating ride as I watched the two of them jump into their newfound faith with vigor, "growing like bad weeds" as my fellow pastor at the time liked to say. Don became an elder. Only five years after coming to Christ, they sold essentially all they had for the sake of Christ. They quit their lucrative jobs to pursue internships in the local church and for Don to go to seminary, in order that they might become missionaries to the urban poor in Rhode Island. That day in my office was not responsible for all of that, but I know that God used that time to do far more than just soak a bunch of tissues.

Don says what softened him that day was not simply compassion for his wife. Nor was it my words or my prayers. It was my tears. He met Jesus in me by witnessing the compassion of Jesus, the God who weeps, in me. He saw this through me obeying Scripture's command to "weep with those who weep,"[159] not because I did so intentionally, but because God had worked in my heart to bring out His image, the image of the compassionate Father.

This is the mighty power of the One who is compassionate and merciful.

---

[159] Rom 12:15.

The Mighty Power of God's Compassion

I am naturally drawn to worship God's power and might as displayed through the works of His hands. God's proclamation of that majesty in the last chapters of Job has been my favorite passage of Scripture for decades. It begins like this:

> Then the LORD answered Job out of the
> whirlwind and said:
>
> "Who is this that darkens counsel by words
> without knowledge?
> Dress for action like a man;
> I will question you, and you make it known to
> me.
>
> "Where were you when I laid the foundation
> of the earth?
> Tell me if you have understanding.
> Who determined its measurements – surely you
> know!
> Or who stretched the line upon it?
> On what were its bases sunk,
> or who laid its cornerstone,
> when the morning stars sang together
> and all the sons of God shouted for Joy?"
> – Job 38:1-7

God continues for four chapters, with imagery of the birth and restraint of the sea and its depths, the clouds and their heights, darkness and light, rain and drought, earth and water, beasts and birds, birth and death. God shows Job His glory, displayed in power we cannot comprehend.

This kind of language, the mighty power of God's majesty, has spoken deeply into my heart since before I knew Jesus. It has taken me much longer to begin to hear the mighty power of God's compassion and mercy. Yet these two aspects work together: in creation, in the fall, in calling and delivering His people, in disciplining and sustaining them, and in sending His Son, not to condemn but to save the world through Him.[160]

To be sure, the Father of all prodigals is mighty because of His vast wealth, because He can command obedience from His servants, and because He can provide robes, shoes, and rings to those whom He favors. He is mighty because He alone can declare what is righteous and what is wretched. He is mighty because He alone can declare a prodigal restored and declare a feast in celebration of that restoration. And He is mighty because He is compassionate and merciful to do all these things.

We are made and called to grow in the image of that compassionate Father. When we see a sufferer, whether victim or perpetrator, our hearts are meant to soften in compassion, to find affinity, to share in his or her affliction.[161] Just as the ministry of presence precedes the ministry of intercession, the presence of compassion precedes the opportunity to comfort. When we have compassion (the English word meaning literally to "suffer with," the Greek implying a melding of the affections of our hearts), we are able to help the sufferer lament because we too lament. Our friend's suffering becomes our own.

Discussion

1. Who do you know who seems especially gifted in the realm of compassion? How do you see that in the person's life?
2. How has God shown His mercy and compassion to you?

Devotion

But this I call to mind,
and therefore I have hope:

---

[160] Jn 3:16-17.
[161] 2 Co 1:6.

The steadfast love of the LORD never ceases;
his mercies never come to an end;
they are new every morning;
great is your faithfulness.

"The LORD is my portion," says my soul,
"therefore I will hope in him."
– Lamentations 3:21-24

Crying out Together: The Ministry of Lament

Discipleship through Lament

> *"Hope and despair are born in the same soil, in the same seedbed. That seedbed is the soil of suffering. The seeds of true hope grow in it as well or better than the seeds of despair, but the seeds must be planted. The biblical laments provide a resource for planting seeds of hope in the midst of suffering. They also provide a pattern for lamenting in a way that does not lead to despair."*
> *- James Bruckner*[162]

Earlier I asserted that biblical lament is strangely absent in our culture. It is very likely that the people we disciple have never seen or participated in this practice, nor do they recognize it or its value. As disciple-makers, we should pass on this neglected gift. We seek to help our disciples join the long line of lamenters who brought their cries to God in the knowledge that He alone is able to hear, know, understand, and act, that He can be trusted to do so, and for that reason we can sing praises even from the depths of our suffering.

Modeling Lament

As with most aspects of discipleship, the biblical lament is something that is best demonstrated rather than taught. This is a terrible beauty within God's gift of compassion: our love for one another causes us to suffer when others suffer. Because we share in each other's suffering, making our friend's pain our own, we can lament rather than simply telling our friend how to do so.

---

[162] Bruckner, 181.

We can do so in the spirit and example of the psalmists, by "writing our own psalms." To review our model of biblical lament in miniature in the 13th Psalm:

1. **Address and petition to the Lord (vv1-2):** Focusing on the Lord as the one to whom we pray, acknowledging that He hears, and asserting our faith in Him.
2. **Complaint describing our distress and request for help (vv3-4):** We describe our suffering and plea for help, crying out with honest and unpolished words from the depth of our souls from our perspective.
3. **Expression of trust in God (v5):** Without minimizing or excusing our pain, we turn to God and express our trust in His existence, power, steadfast love, and faithfulness. We speak truth about our trust in God, that He sees, hears, and answers.
4. **Vow to praise God (v 6):** We now vow to praise God, even if our hearts are slow to follow our tongues. We commit to rejoice in the God of our salvation, making an honest prayer of praise for what He has done and will do.

Our dear friend Karen and her two sisters, Lin and Bev, were extremely close, with Karen and Lin living together for decades. Karen died after a brief but terrible fight with cancer, and we were gathered with her sisters and other close friends and family in a side room just before the memorial service. I was asked to pray.

How do we pray in such circumstances? Grief was heavy in the room, but each person was grieving differently, and my heart was to reach out to each even though I did not know several of them. I had a prideful temptation to say an eloquent prayer due to the four other pastors in the group. In addition, I knew at least one person did not have a relationship with Jesus.

Praise be to our compassionate Father for giving us the gift of lament for times such as this. I paused, took a deep breath, and cried out to Him. I don't remember my exact words, but they started this way: "Lord, this hurts."

"Lord, this hurts." Simple words like these are one way to start biblical lament. As we utter them, we are taking our place in the long line of lamenters who have cried out to God from their suffering. We are addressing our petition to God, acknowledging that He hears, that He is present, that He is able, that He has compassion to listen, and that He will respond. It is the essence of a cry a child makes to his mother over a skinned knee, trusting in her compassion to listen and respond.

I continued, lamenting Karen's death and her awful suffering. I complained to God, crying out how it hurts to no longer have her here. I cried out in confusion, not understanding how her death fits into God's sovereign plans, and not understanding how it could be God's will that Lin and Bev should suffer the loss of their sister whom they loved so much. While I thanked God that Karen was no longer in pain and is in fact living before God, praising His name in glory, and acknowledged that we aren't to grieve as those who have no hope, I still cried out in grief. Crying out to God in honesty destroys falsehoods we learned about Him: that God is aloof, disinterested, or adversarial. Instead, it asserts that God is the compassionate Father who cares, is involved, and considers us not only His friends but also His children. Anyone can be summoned to the throne room of the King, but only His children have the privilege of climbing up into His lap and crying out to Him in honest pain and sorrow.

Then I spoke words that were harder for me to say that day: that I trusted Him, that we know God is good, that He feels our pain, that He hates death, and that He grieves Karen's death deeply. These words were hard to speak, and not because I don't believe them to be true. But sometimes I find that what I know in my head to be true has a difficult time making it to my heart. In such times, I need to speak those truths all the more, proclaiming with my mouth the things my heart needs to hear. In the throes of terrible grief, Job spoke the words, "The LORD gave, and the LORD has taken away; blessed be the name of the LORD."[163] I often wonder how he spoke

---

[163] Job 1:21.

them. Was it with strength and conviction, as if he was preaching a sermon? I do not think so. He just lost all of his children, his wealth, and his livelihood. In his grief he had torn his robe, shaved his head, and then fallen on the ground to worship. I imagine that Job's words were not out of strength but weakness, perhaps barely audible, perhaps preaching to his own heart rather than any other audience. It is important to speak these truths, even if only loud enough for our hearts to hear. As my friend and fellow pastor Matt Furr said to me in a time of my own deep suffering, "There is a place for the jubilant praise of God for sure. But there is something cosmically powerful in whispered praise from the midst of sorrow."

Finally, I called out to God and asked Him that He would receive glory, that just as He had been glorified in Karen's life that He would be glorified in her death. I prayed that the Spirit would draw people to the Father through faith in Jesus, just as Karen had been drawn to Him so many years before. And I vowed that we would praise the God of our Salvation, who has dealt bountifully with us. Again, these can be hard words to pray in time of grief. They must seem strange to those who do not know the grace of Jesus. How can we say He has dealt bountifully? Karen died of cancer, a word I hate almost as much as the disease itself. For days she literally was writhing in pain, pain so intense no drugs could comfort her, at times driving her to lose her normally gracious and encouraging demeanor, lashing out at those she loved. Is that bounty? How can I vow to praise such a God who is sovereign over such awful suffering?

I cannot answer that last question adequately for many. I can only say these truths, truths I believe with greater depth than we could find in the deepest reaches of our oceans. Though I do not understand Karen's suffering in her last days, or for that matter over the course of her life, I know that God dealt bountifully with her. He redeemed her from the pit of the most terrible and tragic of all human suffering, that of our separation from our compassionate Father brought about by our sinful rebellion against Him, the King of the universe. And when His lost lamb Karen repented from that rebellion, there was joy in heaven and God was praised.

> *"The LORD gave, and the LORD has taken away; Blessed be the name of the LORD."*
> *- Job 1:21*

Sharing the Lost Discipline of Lament

Jack Hill discipled me while I was stationed at Sheppard Air Force Base in Wichita Falls, Texas. We met for weekly lunches at a restaurant just outside the base. Being a Navigator, Jack used Scripture memory as a major staple of our conversations. Jack started by modeling this discipline, showing me not only how he memorized Scripture but also how to apply it to both the ordinary and extraordinary events of life.

Jack then walked alongside me, helping me learn and practice this discipline as well. I was reluctant (and lazy) at first, but Jack persisted. Over time, I realized what a blessing it was to store up God's word in my heart.[164] As I learned, practiced, and implemented this discipline, Jack was also teaching me how to pass it on to others. Today, I make it a part of my own discipling relationships and practices.

The lost discipline of biblical lament needs similar emphasis.

Lament can be an individual practice, something that became common in the wake of the Reformation and greater access to individual copies of Scripture. However, historically in both Jewish and Christian contexts, lament was practiced in community. There is a particular strength in this communal practice, even – or perhaps especially so – if that community is only two believers.[165]

Just like Scripture memory, we pass on the discipline of biblical lament by modeling, guiding, teaching, and coaching. As we share in our disciple's suffering and cry out to God, the disciple sees and hears our modeling of biblical lament. Our next step might be to encourage the sufferer to put her or his own words into this form.

---

[164] Ps 119:11.
[165] Bruckner, 181.

Our purpose here is not to speak to the suffering itself, but to help the sufferer learn how to cry out to God in community about that suffering.

This may be very difficult at first. Our culture conditioned us to view complaint as a vice. For the reluctant lamenter, we may begin by speaking the truth of Scripture, in which we see that God welcomes rather than rebukes the cries of sufferers. Psalms 18:6, 34:15 & 17, Philippians 4:7, and 1 Peter 5:7 are some useful verses in this vein. Another is found in Matthew 27:46; Jesus' own example of citing the first verse of Psalm 22, a psalm of lament, from the cross.[166] Indeed, walking our disciple through the entirety of that raw-worded psalm will demonstrate how God does not expect us to candy-coat our laments.

Prompts to assist the person give words to his or her suffering can also help. I mentioned this question earlier: "if your tears could speak, what would they say?" You could also encourage the sufferer to speak to you pointedly and without pretense about his or her experience of suffering, and then ask if it might be possible to speak those same complaints directly to God. Some sufferers I discipled found that they could write their own psalms of lament better than speaking them in the moment. This is a very helpful practice, especially if after writing the sufferer is helped to turn those written words into a spoken cry to God.

At a later time, when the suffering is not as acute or intense, take the opportunity to ask your disciple about his or her experience. "What do you remember about how we prayed together in the hospital?" "How did it feel to cry out to God in such a stark and honest manner?" Then dive into the emotions and thoughts, and do not ignore the uncomfortable answers. Did your disciple feel awkward, fearful, ashamed, self-conscious, or pretentious? What did the two of you learn through these times? How did your understanding of God change? Did you experience His nature and presence in a specific way?

---

[166] C.f. Mk 15:34.

These discussions may in turn present opportunities to discuss the discipline of biblical lament, teaching your disciple about the discipline and equipping him or her to pass it on to yet others. The chapter on lament in Part 1 of this book can help here, using Psalm 13 as a model of biblical lament in miniature. Alternately, consider choosing one of the many lament psalms and working through it together.

Discussion

1. Does feeling compassion for another's suffering seem to come easy or difficult for you? Why?
2. Thinking about specific sufferings of a friend, how could the practice of lament help him or her?
3. Write a lament over those sufferings and share that prayer with the sufferer.

Devotion

Psalm 80: To the Choirmaster: According to the Lilies. A Testimony. Of Asaph, a Psalm.

Give ear, O Shepherd of Israel,
you who lead Joseph like a flock.
You who are enthroned upon the cherubim,
shine forth.
Before Ephraim and Benjamin and Manasseh,
stir up your might
and come to save us!

Restore us, O God;
let your face shine, that we may be saved!

O Lord God of hosts,
how long will you be angry with your people's prayers?
You have fed them with the bread of tears

and given them tears to drink in full measure.
You make us an object of contention for our neighbors,
and our enemies laugh among themselves.

Restore us, O God of hosts;
let your face shine, that we may be saved!

You brought a vine out of Egypt;
you drove out the nations and planted it.
You cleared the ground for it;
it took deep root and filled the land.
The mountains were covered with its shade,
the mighty cedars with its branches.
It sent out its branches to the sea
and its shoots to the River.
Why then have you broken down its walls,
so that all who pass along the way pluck its fruit?
The boar from the forest ravages it,
and all that move in the field feed on it.

Turn again, O God of hosts!
Look down from heaven, and see;
have regard for this vine,
the stock that your right hand planted,
and for the son whom you made strong for yourself.
They have burned it with fire; they have cut it down;
may they perish at the rebuke of your face!
But let your hand be on the man of your right hand,
the son of man whom you have made strong for

yourself!
Then we shall not turn back from you;
give us life, and we will call upon your name!

Restore us, O Lord God of hosts!
Let your face shine, that we may be saved!

Discerning and Responding: The Ministry of Counsel

Why? How? What?

All suffering leads us to ask questions. Why is this happening? Why me? How long? What should I do? As covered in previous chapters, our response to suffering should rarely start with attempts to answer these questions. However, at some point, as we help a person walk through suffering and, as is the aim of all discipleship, grow in the knowledge, practices, and likeness of Jesus Christ, a time will arise when it is appropriate and necessary to provide godly counsel.

Slow to Speak

> *For everything there is a season, and a time for every matter under heaven...*
>
> *...a time to keep silence, and a time to speak.*
> *— Ecclesiastes 1, 7b*

I hesitated to write this chapter, because speaking is something that sometimes comes too easy to us. Time and time again, Scripture reminds us to be slow to speak.[167] Yet we are so often anxious to do just that.

There is a time to speak words beyond sorrow and compassion. There is a time to give counsel. But when we consider how long we should wait before doing so, we should remember that Job's friends sat with him in silence for seven days and seven nights before speaking words of counsel, and they were still too hasty to do so.[168] Our default posture in the face of suffering should be to listen, read Scripture, and pray, not to give advice. As a general rule, instances

---

[167] Pro 10:19, 17:27; Amo 5:13; Jas 1:19.
[168] Job 2:13.

in which a person is in the depths of acute suffering are very rarely the correct times to give counsel.

And yet, there is a time to speak.

It is for good reason that speaking in the face of suffering often intimidates us. We ought to be intimidated, aware of our limitations and tendencies towards the sins that flow from reliance on our own wisdom. The example of Job's friends teaches us that there is danger in providing counsel without God's wisdom. On the other hand, God promises to provide that very wisdom to those who earnestly seek and ask Him for it.[169] We should thus seek wisdom and discernment before seeking the words to express it.

> *"We urge you, brethren, admonish the unruly, encourage the fainthearted, help the weak, and be patient with everyone."*
> *- 1st Thessalonians 5:14 (NASB)*[170]

We entered into, heard, and empathized with the suffering of another. Now this verse and the context in which is it found help us by serving as a starting point for understanding how we can walk together with the sufferer in love and truth, growing in and towards Christ Jesus.

Lead with Prayer

Looking at the verses which follow 1 Thessalonians 5:14, we are reminded that all aspects of discipleship must start with, include, and be followed with prayer. Regardless of our education, training,

---

[169] Jas 1:5; Mt 7:7.

[170] The ESV renders 1 Thessalonians 5:14 as "...admonish the *idle*..." (my emphasis added), but I believe "unruly" (KJV and NASB) get more to the heart of the Greek word ἀτάκτους, "without order or responsibility." See *The Lexham Analytical Lexicon to the Greek New Testament* (Logos Bible Software, 2011) and *Vine's Complete Expository Dictionary of Old and New Testament Words* (Thomas Nelson, 1984). See also the context of Paul's use of the same word in adverb (2 Thess 3:6; 1 Tim 5:13) and verbal form (2 Thess 3:7).

experiences, gifts, or capacities, it is arrogant to think that we can discern a person's heart, much less know how to counsel him or her. But praise be to God that He promises to work through us and to provide the wisdom we need for the work He prepares for us.[171]

We are not replacements for Christ. We are called to stand as His representative and His minister to others. Our duty is not only to share in the comforts with which we have been comforted but also to speak godly counsel, seasoned with grace, out of the abundance of our hearts into which God has poured His love, kindness, and wisdom.[172] We are called to speak words that edify and give grace to those who hear, and sometimes even faithful words that may cause painful yet loving wounds to our friend.[173]

We must prepare and proceed not only with prayer, but also with Scripture. It is the source of wisdom breathed out by God Himself and is useful for teaching, rebuking, correcting, training, healing, refreshing, and guiding.[174] As in all aspects of discipleship, if we are to be discerning and to provide wise counsel, we must be soaked in the Word of God. Scripture does not provide step-by-step instruction for approaching every kind of suffering, but its precepts are sufficient for them.

Another gift God gives us is that of wise counsel from others. It is a mark of Christian maturity for us to know our limitations and to have the humility to ask for guidance from other mature followers of Christ. I acknowledge there are some people with much more experience, insight, and natural gifts in addressing certain areas of human suffering. With permission of my disciples to share their stories, I seek wise counsel. Sometimes this is because I am truly at ends as to how to help, and at other times I am simply seeking someone to test the direction I believe I am being led.

---

[171] Eph 2:10; Jas 1:5.
[172] Mt 12:34-35; Col 4:6.
[173] Pro 27:6; Eph 4:29.
[174] 2 Ti 3:16; Ps 19:7-11; 119:11

The Purpose of Counsel

Our purpose in giving counsel is not to "fix" the grief, but instead to share comfort as we share in suffering. Comfort can indeed mean alleviating suffering (see Jas 1:27, 2:14-17). But comfort does not mean either the removal of grief or placating it with songs, which Scripture tells us is like taking away a person's coat on a cold day or pouring vinegar on soda.[175] Instead, we seek to help our disciple frame the suffering within the Gospel of Jesus, receiving true comfort in the confirmation of God's sovereignty and mercy, and that this sovereign and merciful God is walking with and changing him or her more and more into the likeness of Christ.

Admonishment, Encouragement, Help, and Patience

As with the teacher, so with his disciples. The body of Christ becomes most itself when expressing this Christ: admonishing the unruly, encouraging the faint-hearted, holding on to the weak, being patient with them all. (1 Thess 5:14). This is a comprehensive "counseling" vision. It is tailored for those who need practical assistance: the weak. It is tailored for those who ask for help: the anxious and depressed. It is tailored for those who don't want to change: the unruly. It is tailored for all of us—who usually have a bit of all three characteristics and need a bit of all three kinds of ministry help, who need a lifetime of purposeful patience.
– David Powlison[176]

Powlison wrote often about the usefulness of the counseling model presented in this verse. He emphasized how important it was to discern whether (or where) a sufferer was unruly, fainthearted, and/or weak. Returning to Job's friends, we see how they chastised, corrected, instructed, and otherwise admonished him as if he were unruly, and in some ways he certainly was. Yet if we look at the

---

[175] Pro 25:20.
[176] David Powlison, *The Pastor as Counselor: The Call for Soul Care*, (Wheaton, IL: Crossway, 2021), 38.

evidence we have for Job's condition, it appears the terms fainthearted and weak fit much better than unruly. Job needed encouragement and help from his friends, but they provided admonishment.

Powlison notes that although one condition may stand out as prevalent, sufferers often bear all three conditions in one form or another. As a disciple-maker, we must rely on God's wisdom – soaked in and founded upon prayer, Scripture, and godly counsel – to respond to each. An abusive man whose wife is divorcing him may be fainthearted and weak, but the predominant condition may be his unruliness. Meanwhile, his wife may be in the opposite state: her unruly bitterness concealing her greater struggles with faintheartedness and weakness. Again, praise and thanks be to God that He promises to give wisdom generously and without reproach to those who ask Him in faith.[177]

Patiently Admonish the Unruly

Given the choice, few would choose to disciple an unruly person. Instead, we often seek a person who has similar values, interests, or other personality traits... what we call "compatibility." God does not appear to be interested in compatibility when choosing whom to put before us to disciple. Nor does He seem to honor our discomfort with unruly disciples. Jesus' experience and example were not much different. Judas betrayed, Peter denied, Nathaniel derided, James and John demanded, and Thomas doubted.[178] Each of these men was among His twelve closest disciples who remained when so many others had abandoned Him![179]

The unruly presents the challenge of admonishment with patience. Again, Jesus can sympathize. His answers to Thomas and Philip in John 14 seem to indicate exasperation, as do His chides regarding lack of faith in a storm and regarding physical needs. A glaring example is when His disciples are unable to cast out a demon

---

[177] Jas 1:5-6.
[178] Mt 26:69-75; Mk 10:35; Jn 1:46, 18:3-5; 20:24-25.
[179] Jn 6:66.

(read that again – Jesus' patience is tested when His disciples are *unable to cast out a demon*): "O faithless generation, how long am I to be with you?"[180]

But if we examine both the deeper and wider context, we see how Jesus admonishes with patience. To Thomas and Philip, He admonishes gently and then explains and assures *afterward*. In the boat, He stills the storm *before* He admonishes. In the Sermon on the Mount, He combines assurance *along with* admonishment. And although He is steadfast in His mission and teachings in such a way that many of His disciples abandon Him, in no case, *not even with Judas*, does He abandon a disciple.

Jack Hill noticed my hardened face as I sat down with him for our weekly discipleship meeting. He inquired what was wrong, and I didn't merely open up to him, I dumped everything out. I was angry with my boss, and I had good reason to be angry. My ire stemmed from beyond simple disagreement over policy, but true moral impropriety that was impacting not just me but also his wife and kids whom I loved. But if I was really honest, my more visceral anger was about how I felt *I* had been wronged, and how *I* felt *my* own reputation had been damaged, not the hurts inflicted on his family. I did not speak kindly of him.

Jack interrupted my rant, but not with the sympathy I was expecting. First, he said, "Pat, remember that he is not your enemy. He is the victim of your enemy." That wasn't too hard to swallow, and I could grudgingly accept that truth. But Jack's next words stung, and he started by quoting Scripture. "Can both fresh water and salt water flow from the same spring?" and "The tongue has the power of life and death, and those who love it will eat its fruit."[181] He continued, explaining that my words were like salt water that kills rather than fresh water that brings life. Even though some of my anger might have been righteous, the way I was speaking about a person who was created in the image of God was sinful. Ouch.

---

[180] Mk 9:19; c.f. Mt 6:30; 8:26.
[181] Jas 3:11; Pro 18:21 (NIV).

Jack had patiently admonished the unruly.

We are all unruly at times and in various ways. Powlison offers some helpful principles for giving counsel to the unruly, writing that when sin is specific and clear, admonishment should likewise be specific and clear. "When you need to help someone straighten out, talk straight. Spell out right and wrong. Hold out God's justice, mercy, and power."[182] Such directness presents the unruly with a choice: to continue on the path of sin or to begin the journey of repentance. Our hope for the unruly is the same as the hope we have for the prodigal who lived recklessly and found himself suffering and alone in a field, longing for the pods eaten by pigs. We hope that he would come to an awareness not only of his situation but of his sin, and return to the Father who is waiting to run to Him so that He can embrace and restore him.[183]

Patiently Encourage the Fainthearted

"I can't do this anymore."

I was exhausted more than just about any other time in my life I could remember. I was the second-in-command of a squadron responsible not only for the support functions of an airport and its flying training program but also for the 300 student pilots themselves. About a week prior, I was on the flightline talking to the crew chief about the jet I was about to take up. I saw his eyes shift suddenly toward the runway and I spun around just in time to see a parachute collapse on the ground and fire and a thick plume of smoke rise nearby. I ran from the flight line, dropped off my gear, and arrived at the crash site shortly after the ambulances left and as the firefighters were packing their trucks. The Airfield Manager, a fellow believer, was already there and what she saw was very hard. While we hoped we were wrong, in our hearts we knew they hadn't made it. We hugged and prayed, and then, as I was one of the

---

[182] David Powlison, "Familial Counseling: The Paradigm for Familial Counselor-Counselee Relationships in 1 Thessalonians 5," *The Journal of Biblical Counseling*, 2007: 2-16.
[183] Lk 15:11-32.

handful of officers on base trained as an aircraft accident investigator, I started helping responders secure and document the grisly scene. About an hour later, I was called back to join two other officers and a chaplain as we told the student pilot's classmates that both he and his instructor had been killed. The other officers *and even the chaplain* left almost immediately after giving the news, but I couldn't bear to leave the shocked class alone.

I spent the next week making sure that I looked every one of our 300 student pilots and attached instructors in the eyes to see how they were doing. Both the student and instructor had been gregarious, well-known, and well-liked by many, not just by those in their class. Several of our students and instructor pilots observed the crash from the ground or the air in much closer proximity and greater detail than had I. Most of these young men and women were at the beginnings of their military careers and many never experienced death at all, particularly violent death. I was called in the middle of the night to respond with a chaplain to help one of the students who was in crisis. In addition, I found that many of my 200 non-flying support people had also been profoundly affected and were struggling. A large number witnessed the crash and its aftermath, whether responding to the scene, seeing through a window or from the control tower, or via radio and radar. Others had known the instructor pilot and his family well, and several went to the same close-knit church. Everybody had a story. The trauma was deep, and it was exhausting to be in the midst of it.

And so, at our weekly discipleship meeting when Jack asked me how I was doing, I told him that I did not think I could do it anymore. I knew God had me in this place at this time for this purpose and I wanted to be in His will, but I just could not see how I could carry on this way. I was physically, emotionally, mentally, and spiritually exhausted. I was fainthearted. I didn't have the strength to continue.

As is often the case when people ministered to me in difficult times I cannot remember how Jack listened as I poured out my story to him. I do not know what he said to me. I could not tell you how he prayed. I do not recall what Scriptures he read or recited. But I know all of these things happened because that is how Jack discipled, and particularly how he ministered to the fainthearted. I know he did all these things with patience and compassion. And I know he encouraged me. And somehow, not by Jack's power but by God's power worked through Jack, I got up from that table and walked back into the battleground to be beside the 500 other fainthearted people among whom God had placed me for such a time as this.

Jack had patiently encouraged the fainthearted.

The word translated "fainthearted" literally means "small-souled."[184] Other versions hold it as "disheartened" (NIV), "timid" (NLT), and "discouraged" (LEB).[185] The Thessalonians to whom Paul wrote had plenty of reasons for discouragement, having received the Gospel in "much affliction," suffering at the hands of people including their own countrymen, and experiencing the deaths of loved ones.[186]

Suffering comes to everyone in this life in a multitude of ways and can make our hearts and souls feel very small, leading us to be fainthearted. We may know the path we are to take but are so discouraged and disheartened that we are struggling to walk in it. In those times, we are in need not of a rod but of refreshment. The Thessalonians seemed to be good at this, as only a few verses earlier Paul wrote "therefore encourage one another and build one another up, just as you are doing."[187]

We encourage people not simply with cheers from the sidelines but by coming alongside them, offering them refreshment, consolation, solace, and most importantly, the hope of Christ in the midst of suffering.[188] We acknowledge the person's distress and weariness while assuring him or her of God's faithfulness, love, and

---

[184] W. Vine, et al, *Vine's Complete Expository Dictionary of Old and New Testament Words*, (Nashville, TN: Thomas Nelson, 1984).
[185] The KJV renders this word as "feebleminded," which I don't think conveys the meaning well to a contemporary audience.
[186] 1 Thess 1:6; 2:14; 3:3-4; 4:13-18.
[187] 1 Th 5:11.
[188] Powlison (2007), 10.

strength. We hope to help the person to enlarge their heart not by pulling up on their own bootstraps, but by depending on the God who will never leave us nor forsake us.[189] This is what Jack did for me.

We encourage the fainthearted by representing Jesus faithfully, the Jesus who says to those who labor and are heavy burdened, "Come to me... and I will give you rest." He does not call us to a rest that means the end of the journey. Instead, He calls us to a continuance under His easy yoke and lightened burden, our faint hearts led by the one who is lowly in heart, our souls rested and restored in green pastures and beside still waters. Thus we can be led in paths of righteousness, through valleys shadowed by death, protected and sustained in the presence of enemies, and one day into an eternity in the house of the Good Shepherd.[190]

Patiently Help the Weak

"Sometimes with the weak, the greatest sanctification occurs in those who show care, because the sufferers of weakness don't and can't change much."
– David Powlison[191]

The Greek ἀσθενής (*asthenes*), translated "weak" in 1 Thessalonians 5:14 literally means "without strength." It relates closely to faintheartedness, but where faintheartedness points to fragility of the soul, weakness addresses inability or disability in other realms. This weakness might be long or short-term. It could come from loss such as of loved one, home, relationship, or employment. Weakness may come from injury, whether physical, emotional, spiritual, or moral. It can come through other circumstances and calamities of life into which we are born and through which we live.

Unlike willful unruliness or fearful faintheartedness, which hamper our ability to walk forward, weakness strikes that ability

---

[189] Dt 31:6; Heb 13:5.
[190] Mt 11:28-30; Ps 23:1-6.
[191] Powlison (2007), 11.

itself. A child who refuses to clean his room needs admonishment. The one who wishes to clean her room but fears what might be in the closet needs encouragement. The one who cannot move the dresser to get the sock behind it needs help.

Some of the most repeated illustrations of weakness in Scripture are ones of widows and orphans. In said illustrations, God specifically prohibits mistreating widows and orphans, and commands us to help them.[192] They have a special place in God's heart, with special promises by Him for their protection and care.[193] He even groups widows and orphans with the Levites, His tribe of priests, when it comes to His commands for treating them with generosity.[194] He holds them up and sets them apart not because of their lineage or godly deeds, but because of their weakness, and He commands us to help them.

Often this help has little to do with wise words. We bring meals to the homes of those who are suffering, help with yard work, watch kids, or provide rides to appointments. At other times, a sufferer needs instruction or training. The loss of a spouse, particularly when sudden, comes with the need to learn many, often mundane, tasks. But there are times when those who are weak need helpful counsel.

Nick Clark, my close friend, confidant, and counselor died in 2022. A year later, I asked his wife Kate if she would be willing to share a story of how she has been given helpful counsel in her weakness.

> *I spent a good part of my adult life being comfortable in the role of helper. I had my own personal helper and he was all I needed. My husband was a pastor and counselor and my very best friend. I told him everything and he made it his mission to help me grow*

---

[192] Ex 22:22; Dt 24:19, 21; Job 29:13; Is 1:17; Jer 22:3; Jas 1:27.
[193] Dt 10:18.
[194] Dt 16:11.

spiritually, challenge my missteps, and flourish in areas I was gifted. So I was more than happy to spend my time and energy doing the same for others and I didn't really see a need to build any other significant relationships to provide help for me.

And then my husband died suddenly, leaving me with four children, a ministry, a farm, and a floundering faith.

I had church, I had friends, I had counseling, but the most impactful relationship for me has been my friend, Corinne.

She has listened as I've doubted God's goodness. She has wept with me while we placed a marker at my husband's grave. She has taken my middle of the night phone calls when I can't sleep, or taken me out for coffee and a walk when I struggle to get out of bed in the morning. She has become the person to whom I can tell everything, unfiltered. Sometimes I just need to vent, other times she has gently offered course correction and admonition, and sometimes she has just encouraged me to be in God's Word.

Corinne's godly counsel, willingness to sit with me in my grief, and fearlessness in the face of my doubt has kept me going at a time when it would be easy to give up.

Corinne had patiently helped the weak.

I note that though I asked Kate to tell me about counsel that helped her in her weakness, she started and filled her reflection with examples of how Corinne helped her in other ways. Corinne led with the ministry of presence, being a constant and faithful companion to Kate. She was faithful in the ministry of listening. Corinne was filled with compassion, sharing in Kate's suffering and weeping as she wept so that she could share God's comfort, helping Kate lament.

It is only *after* sharing these many other ways in which Corinne helped her (and there are many other ways Kate would expound upon this help if I hadn't given her limits for length) that Kate mentions Corinne's counsel. Corinne's counsel has been important, transformative, and even life-giving for Kate, but it came only *after* her presence, listening, compassion, and lament.

When the time to speak came, hear how Corinne led with this counsel: by pointing to God and His Word. Scripture is of course where all our counsel must start and end. It is particularly important for this to be the case when we are helping the weak. This is not the time for opinion and conjecture. Nor is it helpful for us to fling Scripture out-of-context and without care.

Also, our counsel cannot be words without actions. As James himself admonishes, "if a brother or sister is poorly clothed and lacking in daily food, and one of you says to them, 'Go in peace, be warmed and filled,' without giving them the things needed for the body, what good is that?"[195]

Quick to Hear, Slow to Speak

I cannot conclude this chapter without warning one more time: **be slow to speak counsel**. Listen, read Scripture, and pray. Sit in the ashes, weep, and lament with the sufferer. But be slow to speak counsel, and when you do speak:

Trust in the Lord with all your heart,
and do not lean on your own understanding.

---

[195] Jas 2:15-16.

In all your ways acknowledge him,
and he will make straight your paths.

Be not wise in your own eyes;
fear the Lord, and turn away from evil.

It will be healing to your flesh
and refreshment to your bones.
– Proverbs 3:5-8

Discussion

1. How has counsel admonished you when you were unruly, encouraged when fainthearted, and helped when weak?
2. Do you have an example of when the wrong kind of counsel was given, even if the counsel was true?

Devotion

PSALM 1

Blessed is the man
who walks not in the counsel of the wicked,
nor stands in the way of sinners,
nor sits in the seat of scoffers;
but his delight is in the law of the LORD,
and on his law he meditates day and night.

He is like a tree
planted by streams of water
that yields its fruit in its season,
and its leaf does not wither.
In all that he does, he prospers.
The wicked are not so,
but are like chaff that the wind drives away.

*Therefore the wicked will not stand in the judgment,
nor sinners in the congregation of the righteous;
for the Lord knows the way of the righteous,
but the way of the wicked will perish.*

Staying close: The Ministry of Persistence

In for the Long Haul:

The infusion room at the cancer center was long, with a dozen reclining treatment chairs set up with their backs against a wall of windows, facing the nurse's station. Each visit we had been favoring the chairs at the end of the room, finding a slice of comfort in the small measure of privacy they afforded in a journey that was anything but private.

Each chair had a television mounted in the ceiling above, but Martha and I preferred listening to music from our phones on our earpieces. Those who did watch TV were admonished by many signs to use the headset jacks. Even when we weren't able to be in one of the end chairs, the infusion room had a quiet and calm atmosphere.

Except when "Courtney" was getting treatment. Courtney always called attention to herself, calling to the nurses as she moved to "her" chair, and loudly making her displeasure known if that one was occupied. Once seated, she would turn on the daytime shock-talk TV shows and turn the volume up to high. Consequently, she shouted over the TV while making phone calls and voice-to-texts, or when giving directions to people about her lunch, or how to arrange her transportation home. I did my best to ignore her, but it was hard.

One day when we arrived, the end chairs weren't available. In fact, the only two that were free were in the dead center of the room. Sure enough, a few minutes after we sat down, Courtney arrived, sat down next to us, and cranked up Jerry Springer. I set my teeth.

My wife, on the other hand, turned to Courtney and said, "Hi. My name is Martha."

Over the next months, Martha and Courtney became fast friends, "chemo buddies." If they were scheduled for the same day, Courtney made sure that two seats were reserved next to each other, and woe be the nurse who forgot or the patient who violated her edicts! Even I lost my grumpiness and began to look forward to the times we would spend together. We learned about her very difficult, abusive upbringing and adult life, her grueling and long fight with cancer, and her beautifully generous and loving spirit that hid below her protective carapace. She even turned down the TV for our conversations. We prayed with her for her health, her son, and her beloved dog. We read Scripture and she surprised us by reciting verses to which she had clung over the years. Martha began visiting her at her home and helping her with errands and shopping.

Martha finished treatment for her first round of cancer in 2020, just as the COVID-19 shutdown began, and though Courtney's continued, we were not allowed to visit her at the center. But Martha was able to continue visiting her at home, and as soon as visitors were allowed again, she was often making stops again to hang out with her "chemo buddy." In late 2021 when Martha's cancer returned and Courtney began to lose her own fight with the disease, Martha continued to visit with her, helping her sister "Jill" care for her in her last days. Martha and Jill held Courtney's hands when she took her last breaths on earth. We held her memorial service at our church and believe she is now fully healed and in the presence of Jesus. Martha is now regularly visiting and ministering to Jill as she grieves the passing of her sister.

The ministry of persistence, by its nature, is often a long and arduous road. But it is one to which we are called.

Often the most difficult time in a period of significant suffering is not the initial onset but the aftermath, as time marches on and life returns to normal for others. We tend to be better at initial response to suffering than to sustaining that care over the long term. Ask a friend who lost a loved one recently, and you may hear that in the days right after the death, the problem was not getting help but getting too much of it. Friends and family have rushed to the scene, asking what can be done and then diving right in. The pastor visited several times. There was a flurry of activity as people pitched in to help plan the funeral, perhaps clean the house, and run errands. The phone was alive with calls and texts. But often, all of that stops the day after a funeral. People leave. The house is empty. The phone is quiet. It is these times which are often most lonely for the grief-stricken, and parallels can be found with other kinds of suffering and loss. Some sufferers contribute to this loneliness, withdrawing from those who would help. Discipleship, however, is a ministry of persistence, and we are called to loving engagement over the long term. We persist. We stay close. We abide.

Persistence Walks

A somewhat tired cliché we might be tempted to fall into is that discipleship is not a sprint but a marathon. I would argue that it is neither. Discipleship is not done at a run, but instead at a walking pace. God made us to be His walking partners. Scripture illustrates the righteousness of Enoch and Noah by saying that they "walked with God."[196] God calls Abraham by saying, "I am God Almighty; walk before me, and be blameless,"[197] and as Jacob blessed Joseph he describes God as "The God before whom my fathers Abraham and Isaac walked."[198] God describes obedience as walking in His ways and promises to walk among His people as their God.[199] As He teaches His people to pass along those ways to the generations which will follow, the essence of discipleship, He describes it at a walking, not a running, pace.[200]

Neither is discipleship a defined event like a sprint or marathon. It rarely starts with a shot or ends by breaking tape at a finish line (save death itself). It is a journey that may be intense at times and less so at others. The journey may slow, stagnate, or even be interrupted as disciples move, wander, stray, fatigue, or become disheartened. There is a specialness to a long journey together, even or perhaps especially when that journey is difficult. As we walk through these times of troubles together, our relationships deepen with one another and with Jesus.

---

[196] Gen 5:22-24; 6:9.
[197] Gen 17:1.
[198] Gen 48:15.
[199] Gen 16:4; 18:20; Lev 18:4; 26:3, 12; Dt 8:6...
[200] Dt 6:7

Persistence Does Not Abandon

The imagery of walking may speak to me strongly because of where I live in New Hampshire, a short drive away from the White Mountains. I am drawn to their majesty, and their vast beauty speaks powerfully to me of the majesty and beauty of the God who created them. My memories of walks in those mountains, particularly with those I love, are precious to me.

But not every walk in the mountains is pleasant. It seems that each week responders are called to search for and rescue hikers who became lost, injured, or fatigued on the trails. One of the most heartbreaking stories that appeared in the news in the past few years was of a man and his two grandsons who were hiking Mount Washington. The 80-year-old grandfather became too fatigued to continue at the younger men's pace. Rather than waiting for him, the grandsons left their grandfather behind without emergency gear or even a phone. After summiting the peak, they descended by another trail and did not report him missing until late in the evening. Rain fell, then as the temperatures dropped below freezing, ice and a dense fog moved in, before being blown out by winds gusting up to 60mph (all common occurrences on Mount Washington, even in summer). Rescuers found the man early the next morning, hypothermic and curled up on the ground in a fetal position. Blessedly, they were able to carry him down the mountain on a stretcher and get him to a hospital, and he survived.[201]

The paths along which we walk with our disciples are much more grueling and treacherous than those in the White Mountains, and we must not abandon them in the wilderness. We are best able to care for, comfort, and support them when we are walking alongside, not from somewhere up ahead. And so, when those suffering slow their pace, we match it. When they become exhausted and cannot continue, we sit with them. When they wander and become lost, we

---

[201] Associated Press, "Hiker Rescued from Mt. Washington May Have to Foot the Bill," (2019), https://www.wmur.com/article/hiker-rescued-from-mt-washington-may-have-to-foot-the-bill/28089803.

search for them. The intentionality and continued nature of a discipling relationship is suited for this kind of persistence.

Persistence Observes

Another benefit that comes from persistence is a better opportunity to observe and assess how our disciples are truly doing. Most people can put on a brave face for a short time. Many of us do this for a couple hours every Sunday. We do our best to hide our emotions, including sorrow, anger, anxiety, and even happiness and joy, from the very people with whom we are called to share and who themselves are commanded to share in both sufferings and comfort. I often joke with my congregation about rural New England having a high prevalence of IFD – "I'm Fine" Disorder. Regardless the depth of their suffering, their response to even the most sincere inquiry as to their wellbeing goes something like this:

"Sam, it's good to see you. How are you doing?"

"I'm fine. Better than I deserve."

Incidentally, I recently received that response from a guy who I knew was in severe pain because he was in the process of passing kidney stones!

Persistence gives us more insight into the joys and sorrows of a person's life, kidney stones or otherwise. It also gives us a better sampling of habits and mannerisms, what a poker player might call a "tell," which indicate how he or she is really doing. It also builds intimacy, making a person more apt to be open and vulnerable.

Persistence Multiplies Disciples

Jesus did not disciple from afar or intermittently. He discipled intimately and persistently. His closest disciples spent three years with him, living in physical and emotional proximity, sharing not only formal ministry and teaching but also the mundane aspects of life. He lived an example of persistence, and not only a persistence in His long walk towards Jerusalem and the cross.[202] He persisted

---

[202] Lk 9:51.

with His disciples even when they exasperated Him,[203] taught them persistence in His parables,[204] and called them to persistence in His teachings.[205] Finally, Jesus assured them He would persist even after His death, saying, "and behold, I am with you always, to the end of the age."[206] Our call to Christlikeness is a call to practice that same persistence.

Discipleship is multiplicative, and persistence is necessary to achieve that purpose. We are called to make not just disciples, but disciple-making disciples; reliable followers of Jesus who will take what they have learned about discipleship to others, and who will in turn disciple others. It is a principle founded in both the Old and New Testaments, persisting in the godly teachings we have ourselves been discipled in so that these teachings will continue for generations to follow.[207]

The ministry of persistence speaks against the flash-in-the-pan approaches of programmatic and event-centric discipleship. It is ministry at a walking pace that teaches the effectiveness of simmering and soaking, what Jesus called "abiding," remaining and walking with, rather than passing through or walking by.[208] God uses our persistence to assure our disciples that they are not alone and that their suffering has not scared us off. As we walk with them, sharing the true comforts of Christ, God is preparing them to do likewise as they disciple others, passing on Christ's comforts to yet another generation of Christ-followers.

Discussion

1. How have you seen God's patience and persistence in your life, perhaps in the form of people He has placed beside you?
2. What are your "tells" that you are becoming impatient or anxious to leave?

---

[203] Mk 9:19; [Jn 17:12].
[204] Lk 18:1-8.
[205] Lk 15:1-11.
[206] Mt 28:20.
[207] Dt 6:1-25; 2 Ti 2:2.
[208] Jn 15:4-10.

3. In what situations do you tend to have difficulty remaining? Are there others in which you feel especially equipped to do so?

Devotion

Be patient, therefore, brothers, until the coming of the Lord. See how the farmer waits for the precious fruit of the earth, being patient about it, until it receives the early and the late rains. You also, be patient. Establish your hearts, for the coming of the Lord is at hand. Do not grumble against one another, brothers, so that you may not be judged; behold, the Judge is standing at the door. As an example of suffering and patience, brothers, take the prophets who spoke in the name of the Lord. Behold, we consider those blessed who remained steadfast. You have heard of the steadfastness of Job, and you have seen the purpose of the Lord, how the Lord is compassionate and merciful.
– James 5:7-11

PART 3: DISCIPLESHIP FROM SUFFERING

Suffering from the Front

Naturally, those who disciple are not exempt from suffering. God uses our suffering powerfully to grow us and those we disciple in Christlikeness. Part 2 discussed our call to imitate Christ by ministering to suffering disciples through presence, listening, empathy, lament, counsel, and persistence. We now exhort those we disciple, "Imitate me as I imitate Christ!"[209] Our suffering not only provides a true-to-life example to our disciples, but also offers them the opportunity to learn to minister in the name of Christ.

By inviting our disciples into our suffering and being vulnerable by sharing our hurts as we model Christlikeness in that suffering, we offer our disciples entry into a workshop of sorts. They can both witness the ministry of the Good Shepherd and join in that ministry. Our weakness bears witness to the Gospel narratives of God Himself taking on the weakness of humanity and His power being made perfect in that weakness.[210] God uses even our sinful responses to our suffering for growth, not just in ourselves, and not just by breaking down the pedestals on which our disciples might place us. We also have the opportunity to bear witness to the God of mercy as we repent, receive forgiveness, and walk in His grace.

Through this endeavor, we have the privilege of witnessing God's work as He causes Gospel growth in our disciples, molding and maturing them more and more into His image. We also gain Gospel partners, faithful brothers and sisters in Christ who have been smelted in the crucibles of both their own suffering and ours, and who can now join us in the ministry to other sufferers, sharing God's comfort with them in their afflictions.

---

[209] 1 Co 11:1.
[210] 2 Co 12:9.

> *How shall we accomplish the great end of our mutual relationships in the face of suffering? Coming to Christ means more suffering, not less, in this world. I am persuaded that suffering is normal and not exceptional. We all will suffer; we all must suffer; and most American Christians are not prepared in mind or heart to believe or experience this. Therefore the glory of God, the honor of Christ, the stability of the church, and the strength of commitment to world missions are at stake. If our conversations do not help people become satisfied in God through suffering, then God will not be glorified, Christ will not be honored, the church will be a weakling in an escapist world of ease, and the completion of the Great Commission with its demand for martyrdom will fail.*
> – John Piper[211]

And, lest we turn this ministry into a mere academic exercise, we must remember that sharing our own suffering with our disciples allows us to avail ourselves of God's gift of grace and comfort in our afflictions, administered through His servants! The wounded disciple-maker is in no less need of this salve than the wounded disciple. Blessed be God for providing this healing gift to us in our weakness.

Discussion

1. Have you ever felt disqualified as a disciple-maker because of your suffering? How so?

---

[211] Piper (2003).

2. What scares you about allowing others to see your suffering? What encourages you?

Devotion

The eye cannot say to the hand, "I have no need of you," nor again the head to the feet, "I have no need of you." On the contrary, the parts of the body that seem to be weaker are indispensable, and on those parts of the body that we think less honorable we bestow the greater honor, and our unpresentable parts are treated with greater modesty, which our more presentable parts do not require. But God has so composed the body, giving greater honor to the part that lacked it, that there may be no division in the body, but that the members may have the same care for one another. If one member suffers, all suffer together; if one member is honored, all rejoice together.
– 1st Corinthians 12:21-26

Growing: Conforming to Christlikeness in our Suffering

Be Transformed

The call to our disciples is "Be imitators of me, as I am of Christ,"[212] and therefore we must seek to conform to Christlikeness in all areas of our life, including our suffering.

Jim Bruckner addressed suffering specifically in the form of illness, but his analysis is applicable to other forms of affliction. He describes three possible outcomes from the suffering. The first is that the person enters "the chaos of illness and treatment" until physical death. The second is that a person is "cured" and returns to the former way of life in the world without learning or changing significantly. "The best imagined result of suffering, however," he writes, "embodied in the laments and Scripture, is that a person will be transformed. A positive life-transforming experience may emerge in the midst of the struggle with illness."[213]

We are called to share in Christ's suffering, and even to rejoice in it. For in that suffering we are being transformed into Christ's likeness as gold is refined in fire. We learn not to follow our worldly desires nor trust on the strength of the flesh, but instead to seek the will and believe in the power of God.[214] Suffering has meaning and purpose, and while we often cannot see or comprehend the full extent of that meaning and purpose, one thing we know: God transforms us through the trials and tests of this world. And as He does so, He also uses our transformation to transform others.

Jesus Acknowledged and Shared His Suffering

"Those who lean in the direction of minimizing pain, or calling for a stoic acceptance of it, are often more precise in their theological formulations [from those who exalt pain].

---

[212] 1 Co 11:1.
[213] Bruckner, 185.
[214] 1 Pet 1:3-9; 4:1-2

> *But they may be guilty of ignoring important biblical themes and thus do not offer the full counsel of God to those who suffer."*
> *— Ed Welch*[215]

Jesus met the suffering of others first-hand rather than denying, ignoring, or minimizing it. He came to address suffering, both the suffering of separation from God and the everyday hurts and sorrows of the world. He felt compassion for those who were suffering in all sorts of ways. [216]

Neither did Jesus hide or minimize His own suffering. He wept openly, expressed frustration and sorrow, was distressed to the point of sweating as if "great drops of blood" were falling, and cried out in agony on the cross.[217] The writer of Hebrews described Him as the Great High Priest who was able to sympathize with us because He had suffered as us.[218]

Conforming to Christlikeness in our suffering means that while we do not dwell in our suffering or ascribe to it undue power, we acknowledge that it exists. We speak truthfully about it to our disciples when our souls are greatly troubled. We confess when we are suffering because of sin, whether our own or that of others. We thereby model Christlike honesty and humility as we call our disciples to do likewise.

Jesus Had Purpose in His Suffering

> *...let us run with endurance the race that is set before us, looking to Jesus, the founder and perfector of our faith, who for the joy that was set before him endured the cross, despising the shame, and is seated at the right hand of the*

---

[215] Edward T. Welch, "Exalting Pain? Ignoring Pain? What Do We Do with Suffering?" *The Journal of Biblical Counseling*, 1994, 4.
[216] Mt 9:36; 14:14; 15:32; 20:34; Lk 7:6; 19:41-42.
[217] Mt 23:37-39; 27:46; Lk 22:44; Jn 11:35; 14:9.
[218] Heb 4:15.

> *throne of God.*
> *– Hebrews 12:1b-2.*

Jesus humbled Himself and took on suffering, bore our sins and carried our transgressions, in order that the world might be saved through Him. He bore our sins in His body that we might die to that sin, live to righteousness, be healed by His wounds, and return to His fold. Knowing this, He did not shy away from that suffering as it increased to the climax on the cross. Instead, He set His face into the wind to endure suffering on the cross not for the sake of suffering itself, but for the joy that lay beyond it, what His death and resurrection would accomplish.[219]

There was purpose to His suffering, and by enduring it He brought glory to His Father and was glorified Himself.[220]

We do not know the specific purposes of each instance or aspect of our suffering, but we know God has purpose in it to grow us and others into Christlikeness, refining us and our faith through griefs in various trials like gold in a fire so that our lives will result in "praise and glory and honor at the revelation of Jesus Christ."[221] Thus, we should not be surprised at nor ashamed of these fiery trials, for they will bring glory to His name,[222] in part because God uses them to transform us into the image of His glorious Son.

Jesus Lamented through His Suffering

> *In the days of his flesh, Jesus offered up prayers and supplications, with loud cries and tears, to him who was able to save him from death, and he was heard because of his reverence.*
> *– Hebrews 5:7*

---

[219] Is 53:4-6; Lk 9:51; Jn 3:17; 1 Pet 2:24-25; Heb 12:1-2.
[220] Jn 17:1-5.
[221] 1 Pe 1:3-7.
[222] 1 Pe 4:12-16.

The long line of sufferers we join in our laments includes Jesus Christ Himself. To practice biblical lament is to be Christlike, and modeling this to our disciples helps them grow in Christlikeness.

Earlier we used Psalm 13 as an illustration of Biblical lament in miniature. In the garden, we see lament condensed even further in His opening prayer. "Father, if you are willing, remove this cup from me. Nevertheless, not my will, but yours, be done."[223]

1. **Address and petition to the LORD:** "Father, if you are willing..." Jesus acknowledges that, in the weakness He has taken on, in His case voluntarily, it is only the Father Himself to whom He must pray, and it is on His will He depends.
2. **Complaint describing our distress and request for help:** "...remove this cup from me." Jesus laments the cup, an image God has used so often as the deserved punishment for the wicked,[224] that it is about to be served to Him.
3. **Expression of trust in God:** "Nevertheless..." Here, Jesus again echoes a common theme from the Hebrew Scriptures of lament of God's faithfulness despite the world's circumstances. "Nevertheless," Asaph writes in lament of mankind's iniquity, "I am continually with you; you hold my right hand... Whom have I in heaven but you? ... God is the strength of my heart and my portion forever." [225] "Nevertheless," another psalmist proclaims, "He looked upon their distress when He heard their cry."[226] Jesus, having cried out in complaint, puts His trust in His Father.
4. **Vow to praise God:** "...not my will, but yours, be done." Jesus vows to give the praise, the worship, that God asks of all mankind: submission to His justice and mercy and to walk humbly with Him, bowing to His will rather than ours.[227]

---

[223] Lk 22:42.
[224] Ps 11:6; Jer 25:15-17; 49:12; Zech 12:2.
[225] Ps 73:23, 25, 26.
[226] Ps 106:44.
[227] Mic 6:8.

Jesus Loved in His Suffering

> *By this we know love, that he laid down his life for us, and we ought to lay down our lives for the brothers.*
> *– 1st John 3:16*

It was for love that God sent His Son. It was for love that Jesus suffered and died. It is for love that the Holy Spirit came upon us. And it is for love that Jesus shared His suffering with His disciples.

> *Now before the Feast of the Passover, when Jesus knew that his hour had come to depart out of this world to the Father, having loved his own who were in the world, he loved them to the end.*
> *– John 13:1*

Thus starts John's account of Jesus' last night with His disciples, in which He served them, ate with them, taught them, and prayed for them. He was preparing them for and exegeting the suffering that awaited both Him and them. "I have said these things to you, that in me you may have peace. In the world you will have tribulation. But take heart, I have overcome the world."[228]

Living Christlike lives before our disciples, serving them, sharing life with them, teaching them, and praying for and with them in our suffering is a way we show Christlike love to them. And again, we call to them, "Be imitators of me, as I am of Christ."[229]

Discussion

1. What were you led to believe about how we should suffer that is at odds with the way Jesus suffered?

---

[228] Jn 16:33.
[229] 1 Co 11:1.

2. What would it look like to your disciples if you were to suffer in a Christlike manner in your current trials?

Devotion

Beloved, do not be surprised at the fiery trial when it comes upon you to test you, as though something strange were happening to you. But rejoice insofar as you share Christ's sufferings, that you may also rejoice and be glad when his glory is revealed. If you are insulted for the name of Christ, you are blessed, because the Spirit of glory and of God rests upon you. But let none of you suffer as a murderer or a thief or an evildoer or as a meddler. Yet if anyone suffers as a Christian, let him not be ashamed, but let him glorify God in that name. For it is time for judgment to begin at the household of God; and if it begins with us, what will be the outcome for those who do not obey the gospel of God? And

"If the righteous is scarcely saved, what will become of the ungodly and the sinner?"

Therefore let those who suffer according to God's will entrust their souls to a faithful Creator while doing good.
- 1st Peter 4:12-19

Inviting: Allowing Others into Our Suffering

We Need the Ministry of Presence

The ministry of presence is something we need desperately. Yet even as we run towards those who are hurting, our pride leads us to erect walls that keep others out of our own troubles. This not only robs us of Gospel care and comfort, but also robs our disciples of the opportunity to grow in Christlikeness through that ministry to us. Jesus Himself, as He suffered grief in the knowledge of His upcoming betrayal, suffering, and death, allowed a woman to approach and minister to Him, and commended her for her great kindness.[230] Later, in the garden, He invited His disciples to join Him and keep watch as He cried out in agony to His Father.[231] Christlike humility encompasses allowing others to minister to us.

Invitation Models Humility

I was blessed to work with people from many different countries. I have enjoyed learning about and experiencing their cultures and have been asked to explain my own. What makes us tick? At some point in this journey, I started suggesting these inquirers read works by President Theodore Roosevelt, starting with his famed 1910 speech "Citizenship in a Republic" (more commonly known as "The Man in the Arena"), given at the Sorbonne in Paris, in which he said:

> *The success of republics like yours and like ours means the glory, and our failure of despair, of mankind; and for you and for us the question of the quality of the individual citizen is supreme.*[232]

With the diversity of culture and thought in our country, many would not align themselves with Roosevelt. However, the rugged

---

[230] Mk 14:3-9.
[231] Mk 14:32-42.
[232] Roosevelt, Theodore. "Citizenship in a Republic." Theodore Roosevelt Association. 1910. https://theodoreroosevelt.org/ (accessed August 8, 2023).

individualism of which he often spoke has been inculcated into our shared national culture for centuries and is hard to shake. We are a self-reliant people, taking pride in the works of our own hands, celebrating the "self-made," and idolizing our self-determination. There is nothing wrong with having or taking joy in a proactive attitude, an industrious will, a striving for excellence, or a job well-done. All of these can be a reflection of God's image into which we have been made. But when we ascribe sovereignty to ourselves and our deeds rather than to God, we are preaching the gospel of self, not the Gospel of Christ. In that false gospel, we ascribe credit for well-being and pin blame for suffering on the aptitudes and attitudes of the person experiencing them. We thus respond to cries of suffering with quips like "well, what are you going to do about it?" It should be no surprise that when the suffering is our own, we are hesitant to share it, lest we be thought weak. Yet we are indeed weak and needy, and suffering proves this truth.

> *Suffering powerfully highlights what has always been true – we were not created for independent living. Suffering exposes our weakness, our blindness, and our lack of control. Suffering preaches that our lives are a community project. Suffering reminds us that God's grace doesn't work to propel our independence but to deepen our vertical and horizontal dependence. The strong, independent, self-made person is a delusion. Everyone needs help and assistance. Everyone has learned at the feet of someone else. Everyone is strengthened by others. To fight community, to quest for self-sufficiency, is not only a denial of your spiritual need; it's a denial of your humanity. Suffering is a messenger telling us that to be human is to be*

> *dependent.*
> *– Paul Tripp*[233]

The false gospel of self-reliance promotes worship of ourselves as sovereign. Inviting others into our suffering attacks that heresy by confessing we are not able to walk this path alone. It breaks our pride, as it is difficult to boast simultaneously both in ourselves and in our weakness.

The false gospel of prosperity clings to fragments of Scripture taken out of context about ability, victory, and deliverance. It diminishes God's glory by making it dependent on our desires for what we define as wellbeing. By asserting prosperity is the natural outcome of faithfulness, it relegates suffering to the faithless. Inviting others into our suffering preaches against that heresy, confessing our weakness and asserting that weakness is indeed normative to the life of Jesus' disciples. In this world we will have tribulation, and yet we can take heart and be content in terrible circumstances, because Jesus has overcome the world and is sharing that victory with those who trust in Him.[234]

Invitation Builds Trust

We have many therapeutic relationships in our lives. We do not go to a doctor expecting her to share her own health concerns, but to hear and treat ours. Discipleship can be therapeutic, but it is not therapy. Its principal purpose is for us to grow in Christlikeness, not to be relieved of our sufferings. And so, while a therapist like a doctor builds trust with a patient through her reputation and results in treating sickness and injury, we build trust with our disciple primarily through a shared relationship with Jesus.

That Jesus is the avenue for building and restoring this trust with one another should not surprise us. He is indeed the means of salvation for all the trust breaking we have done, since that first

---

[233] Tripp, 190.
[234] Jn 16:33; Rom 8:37; Phi 4:13; 1 Jn 4:4; 5:4-5; 2 Co 12:9-10; Rev 3:21.

break of both human-to-God and human-to-human trust when Adam accused both Eve and his Creator in the garden.

Healthy relationships that build such trust involve a pouring out of our lives into one another. As suffering is such a significant part of the life of a disciple, holding that part back stifles the relationship. There are times, of course, when pouring out those sufferings into an already-full cup is not helpful. When our disciples are in acute suffering, they may need us to listen to their cries and point them to Jesus, not necessarily tell them of our own trials. But a relationship that remains a one-way street will never grow deeper. It may be therapeutic, but it won't be the kind of discipleship that helps them grow into maturity. When we invite our disciple into our suffering, we experience a deepening of relationship, a deepening of trust, and a deepening of growth.

Invitation Normalizes Suffering

> *And he began to teach them that the Son of Man must suffer many things and be rejected by the elders and the chief priests and the scribes and be killed, and after three days rise again. And he said this plainly.*
> *– Mark 8:31-32*

> *"I have said these things to you, that in me you may have peace. In the world you will have tribulation. But take heart; I have overcome the world."*
> *– John 16:33*

Suffering was normative in Jesus' life from His birth in squalor to His death in torture. He promised that suffering would likewise be normative for those who would follow Him, take up their own crosses, and be prepared to lose even their lives for the call.[235] Cross,

---

[235] Mk 8:34-36.

tribulation, hate, persecute, kill... the words He used to describe the nature of this suffering were stark and severe.[236] The call to Christ is a call to suffer and to die.

This message is not popular. The popular message, the kind that will fill a 17,000-person stadium three times every Sunday, sounds more like this: "Jesus didn't come and give His life so we could barely get by and live off others' leftovers. He came that we might live an abundant life (John 10:10). 'Abundance' means to have plenty – plenty of joy, plenty of peace, plenty of good health, plenty of resources. Money shouldn't be your focus, but the reality is that it takes money to fulfill dreams."[237] Except that message is heresy, a message designed to tickle itching ears all the way to destruction.

It is certainly helpful to refute such lies with sound teaching based on solid biblical exegesis, but the best counter may not always be rhetoric. There is inestimable power in our personal story, infused with the real work of the Holy Spirit giving glory and witness to our Father in heaven and His Son Jesus Christ, as He walks with us through the valley of the shadow of death. Such work shows that God not only allows suffering or even uses it, but is sovereign over it, even if our "abundance" is not in joy, peace, health, and wealth, but in mourning, warfare, sickness, and poverty. As Dietrich Bonhoeffer wrote, we cannot and must not talk pain away:

> *The poet Stifter once said, "Pain is a holy angel, who shows treasures to people which would otherwise remain forever hidden; through him people have become greater than through all the joys of the world." It must be so and I tell myself this in my present situation over and over again. The pain of suffering and of longing, which can often be felt even physically, must be there, and we cannot and*

---

[236] Mt 5:10-12; 10:22; Lk 11:39.
[237] Joel Osteen, from joelosteen.com

*need not talk it away. But it needs to be
overcome every time, and thus there is an even
holier angel than the one of pain; that is, the
one of joy in God.*[238]

We normalize suffering not to idolize it nor to assign it such a common status that we can easily ignore, minimize, or deny its existence,[239] but because God is sovereign over suffering in such a way that He uses and even ordains it to bring true abundance of joy not in circumstances but in Him.

Through discipleship, we show what it looks like to live as a disciple of Jesus Christ. When we invite our disciples into our suffering, we show that suffering is normal in this life, and indeed a mark of those who would seek to become more like Christ the sufferer. We strip the false gospel of prosperity bare, and bear witness to the truth of the words of Jesus who promises not to spare us from suffering but to walk through it with us.

Invitation Practices Christlikeness

On the night before the definitive battle in Jesus' life, as He prepared to meet not just an enemy, but *the* enemy in face-to-face, mortal combat, these were some of his words:

*"My soul is very sorrowful, even to death;
remain here, and watch with me."*
- Matthew 26:38

The night He was to be betrayed by the closest of companions, before He was to be arrested, humiliated, beaten, whipped, scourged, scorned, and otherwise tortured before being crucified on a cross, Jesus invited three of His disciples to come more deeply into His suffering than the others, to remain and watch with Him. They were

---

[238] Dietrich Bonhoeffer, *Letters and Papers from Prison*, (New York, NY: Touchstone, 1997), 418.
[239] Welch (1994), 4-5.

the same ones He previously invited onto a mountain to witness His transfiguration into glory.[240]

Earlier that night, He invited all of His disciples into His suffering, even instituting a practice to remember it. "I have earnestly desired to eat this Passover with you before I suffer," He said, then over bread and wine He invited them into that suffering. He told them of the betrayal that was in the works, how His body was to be broken and His blood shed, and then said, "do this in remembrance of me."[241]

As the evening progressed, He invited them further into His suffering by saying "abide in me."[242] He then told them that would mean sharing not only in the joy that comes through walking in the great works prepared for us and seeing our prayers answered. It would also mean sharing in the joy that comes from identifying with the prophets and Jesus Himself, who suffered on account of righteousness at the hands of the world He came to save. Lastly, to "abide in" Him is to share in the joy of identifying with those who follow and conform to Him.[243] Jesus invites us come into His suffering, even into His death.[244]

To be Christlike is to invite others into our suffering.

Invitation Teaches Ministry

Don and I were meeting at the diner for breakfast as we had done for over a year. It was exhilarating for me to see this man grow so quickly in the faith. In fewer than two years as Christians, Don and his wife Alyssa matured far more than many others I encountered, and God gifted me a front-row seat to this transformation. During these weekly meetings we would catch up with each other's lives, pray, work through a study, and of course eat. I was privileged to have helped Don work through some very difficult issues and to see

---

[240] Mt 17:1-8.
[241] Lk 22:14-23.
[242] Jn 15:4.
[243] Jn 15:1-25; c.f. Mt 5:10-12; Acts 5:41; Rom 5:3-5.
[244] Phi 3:10.

God's grace carrying him through significant struggles and sufferings. Today, the tables would turn.

"Martha has cancer."

That's one dandy of a conversation starter, but Don already knew something heavy was on my heart. He later wrote of that morning, "I think this was the first time that 'I could barely recognize [you]' (Job 2:12). It was also the first time I would be the one sitting down (Job 2:13)." Don's references to this passage are appropriate, as a predominant theme of that morning and the years that have followed in my relationship with Don is that of a friend who has been faithful in ministering to me by sitting in the ashes and sharing my suffering and grief.

I didn't go into that meeting with the intention of teaching Don how to minister to sufferers. Frankly, I wasn't thinking much about helping Don at all. I needed someone to be present, to listen, to empathize, and to lament with me. Don did all of that and has continued to do that in the years since. And yet, by inviting Don into my suffering, I was inviting him into a workshop in which God would both use Don as a minister of godly grace and teach Don how to minister.

Inviting our disciples into our suffering provides them the opportunity to practice ministering to sufferers, in this case ourselves, in an environment of trust, grace, and mercy. This ministry happens in the context of a discipling relationship in which we are already pouring our lives into one another intentionally, centered on Christ, soaked in Scripture and prayer. We learned to share beyond pleasantries and the deeper sharing of our sufferings allows us to share more deeply in Christ's comforts. The disciple has had the opportunity to experience the ministries of presence, listening, empathy, lament, counsel, and persistence. Now, he or she gets the opportunity to practice what has been modeled and taught.

As with all other aspects of life and ministry we pass along to our disciples, they may stumble out of the gates when first trying to enter into suffering. Your suffering is just as scary for them as it is for you. Your disciple may respond to that invitation in the way we respond to other scary experiences: flight, fight, or freeze. Thus, your first challenge may be to help your disciple learn how to accept your invitation.

Flight. The disciple may initially run away from your invitation, perhaps even finding a reason to cut your time short. He or she might run by denying, minimizing, or ignoring your suffering and changing the subject. This happened to Jesus when He invited His disciples to share in His suffering as He returned to Bethany, knowing not only that His good friend Lazarus had died but also that persecution awaited. They responded by finding reasons to avoid that suffering. "Rabbi," they said, "the Jews were just now seeking to stone you, and you are going there again?"[245] It happened again when Peter denied Jesus rather than taking a risk of suffering with Him.[246]

Our disciples may **fight**. They may respond to our invitation with an immediate flurry of suggestions of how our suffering can be fixed or take actions to do so. Again, Jesus experienced these same responses to His invitation. As He shared His upcoming suffering and death, Peter responded with rebuke, and as Jesus' prophecies about His suffering came to fruition in the garden, Peter fought again, lashing out with his sword.[247]

Our disciples may **freeze**, perhaps quite literally, looking like a deer caught in the headlights. They might not know how to respond or what is expected. They may be unable to process, perceive, or comprehend your suffering. It may be that they just are at a loss of how to respond. We see this in the garden when Jesus invites His disciples to stand watch with Him and pray, and instead of doing so, they fall asleep... three times.[248]

It may help us to be patient as we work with our disciples through these poor responses if we remember how we have done the same.

---

[245] Jn 11:8.
[246] Mt 26:69-75.
[247] Jn 18:10-11.
[248] Mt 26:19-46.

Christlike sharing in suffering is a gift God bestows through learning and experience. As the one He has called to disciple this person, you may also be called to do as Jesus did, suffering even further for the sake of teaching His disciples how to follow Him.

Of course, your disciples might also respond in such a way that you immediately see God's grace and image in them. This was the case that morning I met with Don. When I invited Don into my suffering, he displayed Christlikeness in how he practiced the ministry of presence. He expressed his sorrow. He assured me of his love and of God's. He listened with discipline. I don't think he specifically read Scripture, but I know his prayers dripped with it. He spoke little and when he did, it was to draw out my story rather than interject his. It led naturally to being vulnerable.

Discussion

1. Have you ever been invited into the suffering of a mature believer? If so, what do you remember of that experience?
2. What makes it difficult for you to invite others into your own suffering?

Devotion

Humble yourselves, therefore, under the mighty hand of God so that at the proper time he may exalt you, casting all your anxieties on him, because he cares for you. Be sober-minded; be watchful. Your adversary the devil prowls around like a roaring lion, seeking someone to devour. Resist him, firm in your faith, knowing that the same kinds of suffering are being experienced by your brotherhood throughout the world. And after you have suffered a little while, the God of all grace, who has called you to his eternal glory in Christ, will himself restore, confirm, strengthen, and establish you. To him be the

dominion forever and ever. Amen.
– 1st Peter 5:6-11

Opening: Vulnerability and Transparency

Laying Ourselves Open:

*For thus says the One who is high and
lifted up,
who inhabits eternity, whose name is Holy:*

*"I dwell in the high and holy place,
and also with him who is of a contrite and
lowly spirit,
to revive the spirit of the lowly,
and to revive the heart of the contrite.*
— Isaiah 57:15

Where invitation gives others permission to enter into our suffering, vulnerability and transparency go deeper, allowing someone to see how we are suffering while practicing the ministry of listening. This is more difficult, requires greater trust on our part, and sacrifices many of our idols which themselves have birthed from our idol of self-sufficiency.

Yet James exhorts sufferers not only to pray (which of course would include lament) and to invite the church to pray and minister, but also to practice vulnerability by confessing our weakness and sins to others.[249] Multiple times in his letters, Paul not only pleads for his flock to pray for him, but details his needs and sufferings to them.[250] Being vulnerable and transparent in our suffering casts down our idols of pride and self-sufficiency. Our transparent vulnerability builds bonds of trust and intimacy, normalizes suffering, and helps our disciples both witness and be ministers of God's mercy and grace. Wisdom dictates we discern how we share our sufferings, particularly with the vulnerable and/or young. We should certainly be wary of the temptation to take pride in our

---

[249] Jas 5:14-16.
[250] 1 Th 5:25; 1 Co 1:10-11; Eph 6:19-20; Col 4:3.

sufferings rather than boasting in God's provisions in their midst. Still, whether in our pride or in our shame, we must not err on the opposite side of the pendulum by refusing to practice vulnerability and transparency with those we disciple.

Vulnerability Models Humility

> *Confession that you don't independently have what's needed to walk through the travail on your plate is a gateway to receiving the care that only God can give you through the heart and hands of his people. Hopelessness is the doorway to hope.*
> *– Paul Tripp*[251]

Jesus was vulnerable. He understood that he needed help, and not only supernatural help as when angels ministered to Him in the wilderness.[252] He accepted help from others, including from a man known as Simon of Cyrene, who carried Jesus' cross when He Himself could not bear it any longer.[253] To be vulnerable, to acknowledge that we need help, is to be Christlike.

While I was created in the image of the perfect Father, patient and longsuffering, full of mercy and grace, my flesh hides that image quite well. One of my most persistent thorns, one I have prayed earnestly for God to remove, is that of unrighteous anger. God has done great things in growing me in this area, but it is a battle I still fight. Tragically, my family and particularly my children have been the closest witnesses and often the victims to that battle.

I used to think of anger as part of "who I am." I considered it a matter of how I was created and how I was raised. When I looked back at my angry outbursts and the damage they caused, I focused on how a person "made me angry," and framed the story in my

---

[251] Tripp, 193.
[252] Mt 4:11.
[253] Lk 23:26.

"righteous" or at least "reasonable" response to those offenses. In the initially very rare instances when I took some accountability, I used terms like "testy," "irritated," "snippy," or others that minimized my responsibility. Instead, I sought to gain sympathy, and fell far short of the truth – my anger is sin against the Most High King of Heaven. And just like all sins, my sins of unrighteous anger (which, by the way, Jesus likens to murder)[254] create suffering, not only to others but in my own life as well. Scripture is very clear about what I am to do about this: "Confess your sins to one another and pray for one another, that you may be healed."[255]

I had been meeting with Mike for several years. When I told him about a difficult time I was suffering through with one of my children, he could relate. He also has children with whom he is sometimes frustrated. But there is something far different and far more powerful that occurred when I confessed my sin of unrighteous anger, of seeking comforts not from God but from my own angry outbursts, hurtful words, and self-righteous silence. That vulnerable moment began to reveal *how* I was suffering.

Expounding on the Apostle Paul's report of his own struggles in 2 Corinthians 1:8-11, Paul Tripp writes:

> *We tend to enjoy telling people in detail about the thing we're suffering, while we tend to be more guarded about how we're suffering. Celebrating the gift of the body of Christ in the middle of suffering isn't about reporting suffering but about confessing the struggle in the midst of it. It isn't just about communicating what you're going through but also being honest about how you're going through it.*[256]

---

[254] Mt 5:21-22.
[255] Jas 5:16.
[256] Tripp, 192.

The Apostle invites the Corinthians into his suffering and is then vulnerable and transparent about how he is suffering. He did not reframe the story to appear heroic or a bastion of faith. Instead, he confessed his weakness of faith expressed in despair. He then pointed not to his own strength but to his dependence on the God who raises the dead.[257]

Vulnerability, not simply about the causes or bases of your suffering but about how your suffering is exposing our weakness and dependence, models humility as it topples your idols of pride. As those idols fall, your "confession of hopelessness frees you from attempting to do what you don't have the power to do on your own... frees you from acting as if you're something you're not... robs shame of its paralyzing power... frees you from isolation... [and] positions your heart to receive the gracious comfort that the God of all comfort has promised every one of his children."[258] As Scripture promises, "God opposes the proud but gives grace to the humble... Humble yourselves before the Lord and he will exalt you."[259]

Vulnerability Builds Trust

In the past few years, our home congregation added "pastoral visits" to the ways in which we work to support missionaries. The intent of these visits is to care for our missionaries. However, the visits can add stress for those who aren't quite sure of the visit's purpose. Given the nature of many short-term visits to which many of our missionaries are accustomed, it is understandable for them to have difficulty understanding our request to come calling without an agenda beyond getting to know them and their environments a bit better, to hear their joys and sorrows, and to find ways to share our love and that of our congregation. Our first such visit was to George and Kim, missionaries we met only once and very briefly. They relay how mutual vulnerability helped build trust:

---

[257] 2 Co 1:8-10.
[258] Tripp, 193.
[259] Jas 4:6, 10.

Pat and Martha came to visit us nearly a year ago to the day and we recall our preparations for their visit which would be our first time together in a personal way. Some years previously, we had all been at a large group meeting in their church and we had seen each other but hadn't had any conversations. Looking back, it was in these preparations that the first steps of vulnerability took place, giving birth to the trust that began to grow almost immediately.

We knew that Pat and Martha were facing some important health challenges and their willingness to come and visit "total strangers" was not only courageous but also 'putting themselves out there' to be with us. We realized we were receiving a very precious gift. We had a couple of concerns on our mind. One was for their well-being and how we could make our home theirs and help them feel truly welcome. Another one was if we as missionaries supported by their church would be able to give an experience that would truly help them to know us and the church planting ministry where we serve in Italy.

We met on a video call and talked about how we could plan on serving together in the church in Umbertide, during their stay. Their readiness to serve in any way was encouraging and exciting. In talking and emailing, Pat and Martha offered to bring anything to us that we might want to order from Amazon and have delivered to their house. At first, I was hesitant to take them up on this offer. 'Did they really want to be packing extra stuff into their bags?' was my initial thought. But they both encouraged us to please take advantage of this offer, and soon the UPS truck was making daily trips to their house to which Pat said 'Woot! Woot!' and I knew they were truly happy to serve in this way. In addition to bringing all that we had sent to their house, they brought the incredible gift that was the fruit of a day of work by all of the quilters Martha enlisted to create a unique and one-of-a-kind quilt with Bible verses in both English and Italian lovingly created by ladies of the church.

These may seem like facts that are unrelated to vulnerability and trust. Actually, these very practical acts of love, care, and service were the first steps toward deeper sharing. The kind of sharing that produces vulnerability and trust. The real sharing is the outcome of vulnerability and trust.

Soon after all of the goodies had been unloaded from their suitcases, we found ourselves seated around our kitchen table which became our hang out while Pat and Martha were here. We realized almost immediately that we had a lot in common...which could seem quite unexpected for a missionary couple and a former fighter-pilot become pastor and his wife. Actually, our roles in life were not what gave us commonality.

As we all talked together around our kitchen table, we talked about everything and spent hours sitting together around plates of very simple cookies and tea or sometimes coffee. Gradually, we all sensed we could go from talking about things we do and are involved in to sharing about the deeper things. We shared about our lives, our families, how God has worked in us, what has shaped us, our deepest loves and commitments to God and His Word. We were living the stuff that vulnerability and trust are made of. We discovered that we all had a profound commitment to prayer, to following God at any cost, to speaking truth and to serving Him. We discovered we were all in process on these things and shared what we were learning, things we still need to learn and what we are asking the Lord to do in us so He can work through us.

There were not enough days, but we realized that we can continue to be in touch even through voice messages and share what God is doing as we each continue our walk with the Lord. We pray for each other and share joys and challenges, struggles and victories.

Vulnerability and trust are the essence of a deeper fellowship that is an outworking of

> *God's Holy Spirit in us as we gather around Jesus together. It is a gift that only He can create and one which we are very thankful to share with Pat and Martha.*

Vulnerability Normalizes Suffering

> *Beloved, do not be surprised at the fiery trial when it comes upon you to test you, as though something strange were happening to you.*
> *- 1st Peter 4:12*

When we are vulnerable to share our own suffering with our disciples, we normalize it. God uses our vulnerability to strip suffering of the fear, revulsion, and other stigmas that the world attaches to it. In doing so, we have the opportunity to see suffering as it is: not strange, but under the sovereignty of God and being used for His purposes to transform us and those around us.

Stephen Saint was 4 years old when his father and four missionaries were killed by people with whom they were trying to share Jesus. Years later, his daughter died suddenly of a cerebral hemorrhage the day she returned from the mission field to which she had been called. Many of us would think that his suffering is of a much higher, or even holier, level than our own. Yet Saint says such comparisons of suffering are not helpful. The important aspect is not the severity our suffering but the fact that all of us are sufferers, and this shared suffering in particular enables us to share God's comfort with one another.[260] Moreover, our suffering enables others to identify with us so that they can receive that comfort. Saint writes:

> *People who suffer want people who have suffered to tell them there is hope. They are justifiably suspicious of people who appear to*

---

[260] 2 Co 1

> *have lived lives of ease. There is no doubt in my mind that this is the reason that Jesus suffered in every way that we do, while he was here.*[261]

Indeed, our suffering may specifically equip us to comfort others who suffered in similar ways. Saint precedes the above statement with a recollection of a badly burned childhood friend who was inconsolable until another burn survivor ministered to him. My wife and I found that God has used our experiences with infertility, miscarriage, and cancer to walk with others in similar suffering. He has created, through my experiences, a softness of heart and opportunity to serve those whose suffering springs from military and combat service.

It is not that we must have experience in the exact suffering a person is going through in order to share Christ's comforts. Our shared experience of suffering itself, not experience in specific suffering or lack thereof, combined with our receiving of God's comfort in Christ that equips us to share that comfort with "those who are in *any* affliction."[262] However, God often uses shared or similar experiences to give us special access to and connection with other sufferers.

Vulnerability Practices Christlikeness

> *"If you are suffering because of something outside yourself, it is not that something, but your own thoughts about it, and you have the*

---

[261] Stephen S. Saint, "Sovereignty, Suffering, and the work of Missions," in John Piper & Justin Taylor, eds., *Suffering and the Sovereignty of God*, (Wheaton, IL: Crossway, 2006), 112.
[262] 2 Co 1:4 (emphasis added).

power to put those thoughts away." – Marcus Aurelius [263]

Sometimes, everything in us desires to hide, ignore, or deny our hurt. We take courage in words like these, not from Scripture but from a Stoic. The Apostle Paul debated the Stoics,[264] yet we feel pressure to embrace them in our own suffering. We seek a cover for our wounds, our exposure, and our nakedness.

There was no such place to hide on the cross. Everything about this brutal execution method was designed to expose the victims. In addition, Jesus had been subjected to public scourging, brought before a shouting crowd, mocked by Jews and Gentiles, and then paraded through the streets. The site itself was not in a hidden dungeon or back corner of the city but on a hill for all to see. He was stripped of His clothing, nailed to the beams, and then lifted up further. His clothes were gambled over before Him. People He came to save came to mock Him and just to watch His death. Even His last words to His mother were not private.[265] If one needed an illustration of vulnerability, this was it. Jesus' suffering was on full display.

Even before that fateful day, Jesus did not hide or minimize His weakness. He was honest with it. He shared the hurt inside His innermost being. "Now is my soul troubled," He said to His disciples. "And what shall I say? Father, save me from this hour? But for this purpose, I have come to this hour. Father, glorify your name."[266] He opened up His very heart to them, invoking the words used in great laments of the psalmists, "My soul also is greatly troubled, but you, O LORD – how long?"[267] He was honest with the temptations that

---

[263] Marcus Aurelius, "The Meditations," *MIT Classics*, http://classics.mit.edu/Antoninus/meditations.8.eight.html (accessed September 5, 2023), my translation.
[264] Acts 17:18.
[265] Jn 18:28-19:30
[266] Jn 12:27.
[267] Ps 6:3.

were plaguing Him to be saved, relieved from His mission. Though being God Himself, He took on the vulnerability of flesh.[268]

And then He said, "Follow me." Our vulnerability in suffering practices Christlikeness. And when we practice Christlikeness, we show people Jesus.

---

[268] Phi 2:5-8.

Vulnerability Requires Discretion

"I still have many things to say to you, but you cannot bear them now."
– John 16:12

Christlikeness also includes discretion. At times, Jesus set some limits to what He shared.

Martha and I were at a small retreat with other ministry workers from across the country. The gathering was intended to help us process and heal from wounds that build up over time. The time together included a time to get to know people, and we were encouraged to share our personal struggles. Each of our companions had many real, deep, and significant hurts. They were suffering.

Our turn came. Both Martha and I agreed our biggest struggle has been Martha's continued fight with the return of cancer and all the accompanying challenges. But we also agreed that we weren't going to share that at first. We didn't feel a need to conceal it. Nor was there a lack of trust with these newfound friends in sharing it with them. But we also knew that the word "cancer" is somewhat like opening a hand of cards with a trump card. It shuts down discussion. And so, we shared some real hurts, some real sufferings, but we didn't completely bare our souls. We limited our transparency and by doing so limited our vulnerability. Even later in the week, when we felt it was appropriate to share our struggle with cancer, we held back many of the details of that suffering.

My bet is that our friends with us likely made similar decisions, and this is not wrong! While being open and giving people access to our lives is beneficial, there can be and must be boundaries and limits. Some of the reasons for these limits include:

1. Maturity, both of the disciple and of our relationship with him or her,
2. Triggers and temptations with which that disciple may have struggles,
3. The importance of maintaining other people's confidence, and
4. Our own weaknesses.

Maturity of the Relationship and the Disciple

> *Now when he was in Jerusalem at the Passover Feast, many believed in his name when they saw the signs that he was doing. But Jesus on his part did not entrust himself to them, because he knew all people.*
> *– John 2:23-24*

Jesus, God the Son, knew what suffering He would endure before the foundation of time. Nonetheless, Jesus did not share the whole of Himself, including the depth of His hurt, with everyone. He was initially guarded with the twelve, and even among them had some to whom He revealed more of Himself in both His exultations and miseries.[269]

Trust grows as a relationship matures. Our first meeting with a prospective disciple is likely not the best time to tear away the curtain to the most heart-wrenching suffering with which we are suffering. It is unfair to expect trust to be kept before it is built. One of the many beauties of true discipleship relationships is the process of getting to know one another more intimately even as we get to know Christ more intimately.

This intimacy builds trust, and that trust comes with responsibility on the part of the disciple-maker to assess their disciples' maturity in Christ and in the world into which Christ has placed and called them, and what challenges they are ready to take on. Corrie Ten Boom wrote of a time when she and her father were on a train ride and she posed a question about sex. Her father replied by taking one of their suitcases down from the luggage rack and asking her to carry it off the train. When she was unable to do so as it was too heavy, her father said, "Yes, and it would be a pretty poor father who would ask his little girl to carry such a load. It's the same way, Corrie, with knowledge. Some knowledge is too heavy for children. When you are older and stronger you can bear it. For now,

---

[269] Mt 17:1-13; 26:37-46.

you must trust me to carry if for you."[270] Likewise, it would be a pretty poor disciple-maker who would ask their disciples to carry loads that they are not yet prepared to bear.

Triggers and Temptations

Sometimes our limits on what sufferings we should share with our disciples do not stem from maturity but rather from past difficult experiences or sins of or against our disciple. Lauren Whitman notes that our pain can come from many places; *regret* over our past, ways in which we were *sinned against,* or our *own sinful choices.*[271] Such weaknesses may result in specific triggers or temptations that we must take into account when we consider which of our sufferings to share and the depth and nature of that sharing.

God gave me a special sympathy with and access to veterans who are struggling with the psychological, emotional, and moral wounds inflicted in both combat and peacetime. Those wounds come with certain triggers that vary with each veteran. They might be sensory: sights, smells, noises, even tastes and textures. Others are experiential or situational like phrases or vocal tones, manners of dress or appearance, places or environments, or personal space. The wounds may also come with specific temptations including unhealthy desires for adrenaline, excitement, sexuality, or violence (to include self-harm).

In the early parts of a relationship with one of such sufferers, sharing some of my own experiences in a general manner, inviting them into my own suffering, can be helpful in building common bonds and trust. Of course, sharing specifics of scenes and experiences with vivid sensory details would not be appropriate and quite possibly extremely harmful. Additionally, I must also be cognizant of how sharing even details that may seem benign may affect my disciple's triggers and temptations.

---

[270] Corrie ten Boom, *The Hiding Place*, (New York: Random House, 1982).
[271] Lauren Whitman, *A Painful Past: Healing and Moving Forward*, (Phillipsburg, NJ: P&R Publishing, 2020), 10.

Our knowledge of those weaknesses can only come through the maturity of our relationships, helping us to consider how our sufferings can be shared in ways that do not trigger or tempt.

Maintaining the Confidence

> *"Perhaps these three sieves will help to keep some words from being spoken that would grieve the Spirit of love and hurt someone whom our Lord loves. Is it true? Is it kind? Is it necessary?"*
> *– Amy Carmichael*[272]

The manner in which we make ourselves vulnerable should not force others into vulnerability. We must be cognizant of how our sharing might violate the confidence or reputation of other people by sharing their own stories without permission. Failing to do so may hurt the person involved, strain our relationships, and even open up unintended opportunities for us or others to engage in the sins of gossip or slander.

I spent a good bit of my adult life living in the Midwest and South of the United States, where most people went to church. I also moved every few years, sometimes every few months. It was sometimes easy to share stories in ways that preserved the anonymity of other participants. I have now lived for over a decade (over twice as long as I've lived anywhere in my life) in a town of 2,500 people. The church at which I pastor has slightly over 200 congregants, and is located in a nearby town of 5,000. Both towns are in the least-churched state in the country. The circles in which I run these days are small. It often seems to me that everybody I meet knows everybody else and their business. I have to be far more careful about how I share my story – suffering or otherwise – when that story involves another person.

---

[272] Amy Carmichael, *Edges of His Ways*, (Fort Washington, PA: Christian Literature Crusade, 1955).

Our Own Weaknesses

> "Are they servants of Christ? I am a far better one – I am talking like a madman – with far greater labors, far more imprisonments, with countless beatings, and often near death. Five times I received at the hands of the Jews the forty lashes less one. Three times I was beaten with rods. Once I was stoned. Three times I was shipwrecked; a night and a day I was adrift at sea; on frequent journeys, in danger from rivers, danger from robbers, danger from my own people, danger from Gentiles, danger in the city, danger in the wilderness, danger at sea, danger from false brothers; in toil and hardship, through many a sleepless night, in hunger and thirst, often without food, in cold and exposure. And, apart from other things, there is the daily pressure on me of my anxiety for all the churches. Who is weak, and I am not weak? Who is made to fall, and I am not indignant?"
> – 2nd Corinthians 11:23-29

Paul is indeed speaking of a madman, emphasizing that his suffering should not point to his own greatness but to that of Christ whose power has been made perfect in Paul's weakness.[273] We must remember the purposes of being vulnerable with our disciples; modeling humility, building trust, normalizing suffering, and practicing Christlikeness. Concurrently we must remain aware of our own weaknesses, which fight against said purposes.

---

[273] 2 Co 12:9.

Since the garden, mankind has used for evil the very things that God made very good in our pursuit of "all that is in the world – the desires of the flesh and the desires of the eyes and the pride of life."[274] It is tempting for us to use our suffering as an opportunity to express our pride and pursue our passions.

We should indeed, as Paul did, boast of our weakness. However, we must do so remembering and asserting that the hero of our story is the Jesus, the Suffering Servant Himself who meets us in our sorrows, rather than lionizing ourselves in His place. God uses our suffering to humble and even break us as He grows us into the likeness of, not the replacement for, our Savior. If our story does not point us and those around us to Christ, it is vanity. It is then not vulnerable humility but self-aggrandizing pride. "If I must boast," Paul continues, "I will boast of the things that show my weakness."[275] The response to the vulnerable sharing of our suffering should not be "what a great person you are to suffer such," but "what a great God and Savior you have."

Discussion

1. What do we risk by making ourselves vulnerable in our suffering to a disciple?
2. How could humble and wise vulnerability and transparency in your suffering help your disciple grow in Christlikeness?

Devotion

I am poured out like water,
and all my bones are out of joint;

my heart is like wax;
it is melted within my breast;

---

[274] 1 Jn 2:16.
[275] 2 Co 12:30.

my strength is dried up like a potsherd,
and my tongue sticks to my jaws;
you lay me in the dust of death.

For dogs encompass me;
a company of evildoers encircles me;
they have pierced my hands and feet—

I can count all my bones—
they stare and gloat over me;

they divide my garments among them,
and for my clothing they cast lots.
– Psalm 22:14-18

Modeling: Suffering as Witness to the Gospel of Christ

Pointing to Jesus

It bears repeating that our suffering should point to Christ. Perhaps the most powerful discipleship tool we have is our living witness to the Gospel of Christ as we journey through times of suffering. While we desire that this witness to the Gospel be godly, praise God that in His sovereignty, He uses even our weak and stumbling faith for His glory. The most prominent sufferings my wife and I experienced fall into three areas: infertility and miscarriage, loss of family and friends, and cancer. In each of these, we know that God granted us times of extraordinary faithfulness, a faithfulness He has used to grow us and others in Christlikeness. Conversely, there have also been times of great failings, fallings, and unfaithfulness. God, in ways only the sovereign King can do, used the latter times of failing just as powerfully, often through the witness of the process of confession, repentance, and restoration. As we witness to our disciples through suffering, we also offer them the opportunity to come alongside and even lead and counsel us in lament, confession, and repentance.

Godly Suffering as Witness

Tim and the three other members of his crew died in an aircraft crash one terrible night over thirty years ago. He was the first of many military friends I would lose. After the formal memorial service, my wife and I attended a civilian service at his church where Tim's wife Beth stood up before a packed room of family, friends, and strangers to give a eulogy.

I was young and immature in my faith. Besides my grandfather and some more distant relatives, I had very little exposure to death and mourning. I was struggling to comprehend the thoughts and feelings I was experiencing. I simply couldn't grasp how Beth, a woman suddenly widowed at an age when marriage seems to be all about life, could stand up and speak in a moment like this, in such deep suffering, and especially in front of so many.

It was many years later when I learned that "eulogy" comes from the Greek "to speak well," referring to our tradition of remembering the deceased by speaking well of them. Beth spoke well, but it is not her eulogy of Tim I remember, it is how she eulogized his Savior. "Tim would want you to know..." she said, and then followed with a clear, passionate, and compelling proclamation of the Gospel message, from creation to fall to redemption to restoration, and an invitation to join Tim not in his death, but in Christ's.

Sadly, and yet miraculously and wonderfully, I have since observed many more widows, widowers, parents, children, and others witness through their godly suffering in death's wake. They borne witness not to their own strength but to the sufficiency of their Savior. There is a special persuasive power in the witness of one who cries out, not denying or ignoring their pain and loss, in praise of the God who not only welcomes his children into eternal life but walks with them in their suffering during the days of their life on this earth.

This power of witness is not confined to those who suffer the death of loved ones. Godly suffering – in illness, injury, loss, discouragement, and all other kinds of pain – is a witness to the God who suffers, weeps, hears, responds, acts, knows, and is present.

Human Weakness as Witness

> *"The credit belongs to the man who is actually in the arena, whose face is marred by dust and sweat and blood; who strives valiantly; who errs, who comes short again and again, because there is no effort without error and shortcoming..."*
> *– Theodore Roosevelt*[276]

---

[276] Roosevelt, Theodore, "Citizenship in a Republic." Theodore Roosevelt Association, 1910, https://theodoreroosevelt.org/ (accessed August 8, 2023).

A dear friend and widow once told me how much she dislikes being called "amazing." She does not feel amazing. She struggles to parent, to run a household, to work, and sometimes even to breathe. When people call her "amazing," she feels as if she is expected to be superhuman when she just wants to grieve like anyone who has lost her husband, her life partner, the father of her children, and her best friend. She isn't superhuman. She is weak.

Yet there is something about exposed human weakness that amazes us. President Roosevelt was correct when he said that our adoration is not for the strong person who succeeds in all his ventures, but rather the "war-worn Hotspur, spent with hard fighting, he of the many errors and the valiant end, over whose memory we love to linger."[277] Shakespeare's Hotspur does not stand alone in our memories. Recall the many stories, novels, and movies – from the Ugly Duckling and Cinderella to Rocky and Braveheart – that feature suffering protagonists for whom we cheer as they are struck to the ground and then struggle back to their feet. We are drawn to the suffering underdog.

Where most of these stories get it wrong is in ascribing credit. The credit does not belong, as Roosevelt declared, to the one in the arena. It instead belongs to the God whose grace is made perfect in human weakness, whose strength is the one on which the weak one falls, to whom the helpless commits himself, who has always been the helper of the fatherless and the hearer of the afflicted.[278] He is the one who is amazing.

Our weakness is itself a witness to God and His Gospel. Do not hide it from your disciples. Be honest with them. Boast of your weakness so that you can boast of God's amazing grace made perfect in it. Show them how you have stumbled, failed, erred, and come up short. Throw your pitifully weak self on the merciful strength of God and teach others to do likewise.

---

[277] *Ibid.*
[278] Ps 10:14, 17; Is 40:29-31; 2 Co 12:9.

Biblical Lament as Witness

*When peace like a river attendeth my way,
when sorrows like sea billows roll;
whatever my lot, thou hast taught me to say,
"It is well, it is well with my soul."*[279]

Our lament in suffering is likewise a witness to the Gospel of Christ. Each element of lament testifies to the God who is unlike any god mankind has conjured. Where the gods of mankind are indifferent or indignant toward the cries of their subjects, our God not only allows raw wailing, but encourages and even commands it. The gods of the world are aloof while our God can be trusted to heal the brokenhearted and binds up their wounds.[280] The gods made by human hands demand worship in the form of sacrifices, but the God of heaven calls us to worship by walking in justice and kindness with the one who has dealt bountifully with us.[281]

Though I do not relish funerals at all, they present a paramount opportunity to proclaim the Gospel to those who do not know it. At our church, as I observed in others, we commonly start a funeral service with an explanation of what we are doing. Lament over a believer's death makes no sense in contemporary Western culture. It grieves much differently because it is bereft of true hope.[282] And so, we explain how it is possible both to grieve and rejoice over the death of our brother or sister. We then cry out, weep, sob, and express our deep grief at the tragedy of death and the sin that brought it into the world. We speak the truth that sorrows are rolling through our life like the relentless waves of the sea. And we also sing praises to the God of our salvation, rejoicing in His providence and provision, and taking solace in the peace that attends our ways like a steady river of fresh water. This lament – crying out

---

[279] Horatio Gates Spafford, "It Is Well with My Soul" (1873).
[280] Ps 147:3.
[281] Ps 13:6; Mic 6:8.
[282] 1 Th 4:13-18.

in our pain while trusting in our God – is a powerful witness to the Gospel of Christ.

Gospel Repentance as Witness

> *What patience would wait as we constantly roam*
> *What Father, so tender, is calling us home*
> *He welcomes the weakest, the vilest, the poor*
> *Our sins they are many, His mercy is more.*[283]

There was a stretch early in our married life during which suffering, some of which I already mentioned, seemed especially acute for Martha and me. We lost close friends and family members to accidents, sickness, and suicide. We lost our first child's life and almost Martha's to miscarriage. We were struggling with infertility. Frequently, I responded to this suffering by turning to anger and bitterness instead of turning to Christ.

I returned home from work after a banner day. In my self-righteous anger, I managed to chew out my flight commander before storming out of his office. Usually, this is not a career-enhancing move, but I am ashamed to admit that my outbursts were so regular that I think he just shrugged it off. In the hallway, I ran into my aircraft commander, a good friend, who stopped me to offer an additional duty that most would consider to be a very good opportunity. In thanks, I lambasted him for having the audacity to ask me to do anything extra for the squadron. After my short drive home, I pridefully described the events and offenses of the day to Martha. I don't think she said anything in response. She had become sadly accustomed to my destructive behavior and already reached out to our pastor and others for help.

That evening, like the prodigal son, I "came to myself." I don't know what spurred the reflection, but I realized that I was a self-righteous, angry, bitter hypocrite who was sinning against God and

---

[283] Matt Boswell and Matt Papa, "His Mercy is More" (2016).

against people made in His image. I was presenting myself as a follower of Christ while living a life that was a dishonor to His holy name. I was hurting my witness, and I was hurting everybody around me. I had been oblivious to my wife's suffering, which was greater than mine in every aspect. Rather than growing with her in faith, I had drawn her into bitterness and despair. I was blind to the suffering of my comrades-in-arms who lost some of the same friends. And I had been oblivious to the way I squandered opportunities to proclaim the Gospel of grace because I was so preoccupied proclaiming my self-righteous anger.

The next morning, I knocked at the door of my Squadron Commander's office. I still remember his hesitant look as he invited me in, no doubt expecting me to present my latest grievance. Instead, I said, "Sir, I'm sorry." I explained how I knew that he, as the commander, shouldered far more burden than I had in the loss of our friends and the care of their families, and that instead of helping him, I made his life even more difficult with my behavior and attitudes. I told him I was very sorry for this, and that I was going to change. I don't know how long his jaw stayed open after I left. From there, I went on to apologize to my flight commander, my aircraft commander, and others.

It was a turning point in my life, though the progress was very slow at first, and I still refer to that time as "the dark years." Yet over time, God changed me. I still struggle with this sin, but God taught me to turn to Him more and more. When I do fall, He helped me to repent more readily and more completely. As I relayed my struggles to a Christian brother I have been privileged to get to know quite intimately over the past year, he said, "Pat, I want you to know that I don't think of you as an angry man." Praise be to God. Nonetheless, I still feel deep regret and guilt for how terribly my sin tarnished my witness to Christ and how it still does when I fall back into those sinful patterns.

A few years ago, my wife and I received a Christmas card from a couple we knew during those dark years. They wrote that they became followers of Christ, and wanted us to know that God had used our witness to bring them to saving faith. We cried in a mixture of joy, wonder, and confusion. We were unable to understand how they could have perceived the truth of the Gospel in our fallen lives. This past year, that couple visited us. As we heard them tell their journey of faith, we were amazed at how God had used our witness in it. He didn't use a perfect witness, and not even a pretty witness. He used the witness of us wrestling with Him, falling into sin, crying out in despair, repenting, and then continuing that cycle – wrestling, falling, crying, repenting...

Our God redeems broken people with broken people.

Our witness is indeed tarnished when our disciples see us respond to the heat of suffering with sinful thorns rather than Christ-honoring fruit.[284] Praise be to God that His grace is made perfect in our weakness, and that the confession and repentance with which He gifts us are so much more powerful than even our worst sins. Our sins are indeed many, but His mercy is more.

God's Mercy and Grace as Witness

> *But unless we make space for grief, we cannot know the depths of the love of God, the healing God wrings from pain, the way grieving yields wisdom, comfort, even joy."*
> *– Tish Warren*[285]

The beauty of repentance is in the mercy and grace with which God responds to it. He does not gloat, does not condemn, and does not shun. Instead, our compassionate Father sees us while we are yet a long way off, and responds to our repentance by running to us, embracing us, kissing us, and restoring us.

He proclaims His mercy and grace in His Scriptures, and through our redeemed lives. There is nearly inexplicable power in the one who relies not on His or her own strength, but on the redemptive

---

[284] Nichols & Thorne.
[285] Tish Harrison Warren, *Prayer in the Night: For Those Who Work or Watch or Weep*, (Downers Grove, IL: InterVarsity Press, 2021), 43.

power of Christ. We do not ignore our suffering, deny it, or even rush through it. At the same time we do not dwell in its depths as those who have no hope. Having invited our disciples into our suffering, opened our hearts in vulnerability to that suffering, allowed them to minister to us and lament with us, and then confessed our sins before them, we now share the power that comes only through faith in Christ. We embrace His forgiveness and move forward in redemption, not depending on the improvement of our earthly circumstances. Rather, we trust that God is using our suffering to change us and others from one degree of glory to another. We share in Christ's sufferings, we share in His comfort, and we will share in His glory.

Discussion

1. How did you grow deeper in your understanding and apprehension of the Gospel through observing the suffering of others?
2. How do you respond to the idea that that God may be purposing your suffering to be a witness to others?

Devotion

So then, brothers, we are debtors, not to the flesh, to live according to the flesh. For if you live according to the flesh you will die, but if by the Spirit you put to death the deeds of the body, you will live. For all who are led by the Spirit of God are sons of God. For you did not receive the spirit of slavery to fall back into fear, but you have received the Spirit of adoption as sons, by whom we cry, "Abba! Father!" The Spirit himself bears witness with our spirit that we are children of God, and if children, then heirs—heirs of God and fellow heirs with Christ, provided we suffer with him in order that we may also be glorified with

him.
– Romans 8:12-17

Teaching: Passing on What We Have Learned

Make Disciple-Making Disciples

> *"And these things which you have heard me say in the presence of many, entrust to reliable men who will be able to teach others also."*
> *- 2nd Timothy 2:2*

The Navigators use this verse to express the concept of discipleship over multiple generations. We pass on Gospel truths to our disciples intending that they will in turn disciple others. We should also encourage and exhort our disciples to take what they learned and how they have grown and pass it on to those who will be able to continue this call to disciple-making.

Discipleship is much more than teaching others what we know, but it is not less than that either. As we walk through our own suffering and the suffering of others, we learn about God and come to know Him better. It is important that we pass these lessons on. Just as we might prepare to teach other lessons, we should record our experiences, apply Scripture and prayer to our observations and thoughts, and work to present lessons in an organized and accessible manner. I find that the discipline of journaling, particularly during my morning devotions, to be a key part of this process, if for no other reason than pen and ink represent a more permanent and reliable storage media than my own memories.

Demonstrating

One of the first and most important ways we teach disciples how to disciple a sufferer is through *showing* them, through our own ministry to them in their suffering. As we are present in their suffering, entering into their suffering, and practice the disciplines of listening, empathy, lament, counsel, and persistence, we are not only ministering to them but we are teaching them what it means to be a minister of Christ's grace.

We also demonstrate this ministry by walking with our disciples so that they can observe how we minister to others.

When I arrived at our breakfast meeting, Don explained that he managed to secure another table back in a more private corner instead of the middle of the diner where "Mia" tried to seat us. I told him I was just fine with that and sat down, putting my Bible on the table along with one of the black bound notebooks I became accustomed to keeping with it. Sometime later, Mia stopped by and asked if we would please pray for her son. I said I would, asked for his name, and wrote it in my notebook as I inquired what was going on. She started slowly, telling us about her young son being sick, but soon opened up further about other troubles he was having as well as difficulties she was having with his father. I asked if it would be OK for us to pray now, and she said yes.

Later as we were eating, two men seated near us got up and stopped by our table on their way out. One introduced himself as a fellow believer and thanked us for praying for Mia and for our witness in studying the Bible in public.

Don is much more tech savvy than I am and takes most of his notes on a tablet with a keyboard in its cover. At our next meeting, however, Don too had a notebook. When Mia came to the table, he asked her how her son was doing, and took notes as she spoke about how to pray for her. After she left, he explained that the previous meeting changed his perspective in several ways. He was initially apprehensive when I offered to pray for Mia. Pray? In front of all these people? Next, he told me how he observed Mia's demeanor change when I started taking written notes. Finally, he described how surprised he had been when the man was encouraged rather than offended by our prayer and study (remember, New Hampshire is the least-churched state in the country). Over the next weeks and months, I took great joy in letting Don take the lead in ministering to Mia in prayer and in sharing the Gospel.

Through this experience and many others, I came to learn that while our disciples do indeed learn through what we say, what they observe is perhaps even more powerful. I had not been trying to teach Don about how to enter into, listen, or respond to suffering. I was simply imitating what I learned from observing and listening to others before me, and Don began to imitate me. Often, that is how discipleship works.

Explaining

In addition to demonstrative guidance, Jesus also taught by explaining what He was doing and what He had done. As He was ministering to His disciples by washing their feet, Peter resisted, and Jesus explained a little about what He was doing. And then, when He was finished washing their feet, He expounded, starting by saying, "Do you understand what I have done to you?"[286]

Similarly, opportunities to teach may arise in the midst of our ministry to a suffering disciple, and not only through our counsel. Given our neglect of biblical lament, it may help to explain (briefly!) what we are doing in the moment. For example:

"James, I don't have answers for those questions, but I've been learning a lot lately about something called lament, how people in the Bible cried out to God. Could I show you how I am learning to put this into practice?"

Our persistence will yield subsequent opportunities to teach more fully, to answer more complex questions, and to pass along what we learned. This may come through questions from our disciples, as it did when I asked Father Mike what he had done for us in the hospital room and he took the time to teach me about the ministry of presence.

Sending

In 1933, a man named Dawson Trotman was meeting one-to-one with a Navy sailor named Les Spencer, teaching him to study and memorize the Bible and share the Gospel with others. One day, Les brought a shipmate to their meeting. The shipmate was interested in how Les' life had changed, and Les asked Dawson if he would

---

[286] Jn 13:3-20.

teach the man what he had taught Les. Dawson replied, "You teach him!" Les did, and then the two sailors began meeting with others on their ship. By the time they were done, 125 men on the crew of the U.S.S. West Virginia were growing in Christ. By the end of World War II, thousands in the military and civilian life were participating in this discipleship ministry known as "The Navigators."[287]

A key principle of discipleship is the practicing and passing on what has been learned, whether how to study our Bibles, how to pray, or how to share comfort with a sufferer. Having ministered to our disciples in their suffering, welcomed them into ours, and perhaps even helped them to observe how we minister to others, the next step is to send them off to do likewise. Since suffering is common to all mankind, your disciple won't have to look far for a place to serve.

Sending your disciple to disciple others does not imply we "launch and leave." My disciplers certainly did not do that with me. As I took my first steps and missteps, they were there to hear my questions, provide counsel, and most importantly, pray for me. I still use the "phone a friend" option quite often, and not just with situations that are "difficult" or different. As with any other practice, our disciples will need and likely appreciate assurance, exhortation, and encouragement as they go on to imitate us as we imitate Christ.

Discussion

1. Over time, we learn that just as each of us has our own preferred learning style, we also have a preferred style of teaching. How would you describe yours?
2. Do you remember one of the first times you passed along something you learned to someone else? How would you describe that experience?

---

[287] https://www.navigators.org/resource/the-wheel-illustration/ (accessed August 17, 2023).

Devotion

> *[18] And Jesus came and said to them, "All authority in heaven and on earth has been given to me. [19] Go therefore and make disciples of all nations, baptizing them in the name of the Father and of the Son and of the Holy Spirit, [20] teaching them to observe all that I have commanded you. And behold, I am with you always, to the end of the age."*
> *– Matthew 28:18-20*

CONCLUSION

Ed Welch wrote that we are both needy and needed.[288] Our suffering and our sin render us needy of salvation, not only into eternity but also in this present world. God sent Jesus into the world to save us from not only the most awful of all human suffering – the eternal separation from our loving Father we have earned through our sin, but also to save us in this life. In our fallen world, Jesus saves us not by removing us from suffering but walking through it with us, just as He called us to do since the beginning. Having walked through tribulations with His disciples, walked to the cross, and then rose from the grave to walk with those disciples again, He said, "and behold, I am with you always, to the end of the age."[289]

But then He left. He ascended into heaven. How is that "with" us?

One answer to this question is that Jesus, God the Son, when He returned to God the Father, sent God the Holy Spirit, the One He called "the Helper," to teach His disciples all things, guide them in the truth, declare to them the things to come, to empower, exhort, encourage, gift, strengthen, convict... and, to be with them and in them forever.

Another answer to this question is found in Jesus' command just before He made that promise. "Make disciples." By the power of the Holy Spirit, they were to make disciples who would themselves receive the Holy Spirit. They were to make disciples who observed all that He commanded His first disciples, and that of course included making more disciples. Make disciples who will represent Jesus to others, to walk beside them, sharing in suffering and sharing in comfort.

We are needed because Jesus is needed.

---

[288] Welch (2015), 11-13.
[289] Mt 18:20.

APPENDIX

Suggested Scriptures

In addition to the Scripture below, you might consider some of the passages I've included in the "Devotion" portion of each chapter.

Psalter

The following list is an excerpt from the topical selection of psalms in the 2019 Anglican Book of Common Prayer.[290] Note that they are not all in numerical order, but generally in precedence of the compilers' view of pertinence to the respective topic.

God's Sovereignty:

24, 93, 46, 47, 72, 89, 96, 97, 98, 99, 112, 146, 145

God's Mercy:

23, 100, 32, 130, 57, 61, 62, 63, 73, 77, 85, 86, 103, 118, 145

Trust in God

27, 31, 57, 147, 62, 63, 71, 73, 77, 91, 118, 121, 124, 125, 123, 143

God our Refuge

4, 20, 17, 37, 46, 49, 54, 61, 71, 91, 103, 121, 146

Peace

29, 46, 76, 85, 98, 100, 124, 125, 126

The Transitoriness of Life:

39, 49, 90

---

[290] The Anglican Church of North America, *The Book of Common Prayer*, (Huntington Beach, CA: Anglican Liturgy Press, 2019), 269.

Weborg's Psalms

Though many of my seminary notes are collecting dust, I have kept a list of psalms compiled by Professor C. John Weborg close at hand. The last two topics particularly are ones I have not often seen included in other resources.

Penitential/Confession of Sin

6, 38, 32, 51, 102, 130, 142

God's Consolation

23, 27, 34, 37, 62, 85

Individual Lament

13, 17, 22, 38, 42, 44, 56, 69:9-13, 73:1-9 & 21-26, 77, 88, 142

Communal Lament

56, 73, 123

Psalms of Anger

35, 52, 55, 57, 59, 69, 79, 83, 94, 109, 137, 140

Acquiring Wisdom in Suffering

26, 37, 49, 73, 82, 94

Scriptures for Suffering

Again, I have leaned on the Anglican Book of Common Prayer, particularly in its excellent liturgies for ministering to the sick and the dying,[291] for some of these suggestions while adding my own.

General

Psalm 23; Matthew 6:9-13 (The Lord's Prayer); John 3:16-21; Ephesians 2

---

[291] *Ibid*, 225-245.

In Sickness

Psalms 62; 103; 145; John 3:16-21

Perseverance

Psalm 91; Isaiah 53; 1st Peter 2:21-25; 1st Thessalonians 5:16-24, 2 Corinthians 12:7-10; Romans 8:18-39

Hope in Healing

2nd Kings 5:1-14; James 5:13-20; Luke 5:12-26; Luke 13:10-17; Acts 3:1-10

Hope of Eternity

Luke 2:25-35; John 14; 1st Corinthians 15:42-58; 2nd Corinthians 4:7-18; 1st Thessalonians 4:13-18

Ministering to the Dying

John 14:1-7; 1st Corinthians 5:54-57; Revelation 21:1-7; Luke 2:29-32 (Simeon's Song)

Grieving Death

Psalm 121; 1st Thessalonians 4:13-15; John 14:1-7; Revelation 21:1-7

Grieving Loss of Dreams

Lamentations 3:1-24; Matthew 11:2-6; Ruth; Genesis 37

Grieving Loss of Livelihood

Psalm 126:1-6; Philippians 4:4-7, 10-13; Hebrews 13:5-6

BIBLIOGRAPHY

Alden, Robert L. *Job*. Nashville, TN: Broadman & Holman Publishers, 1993.

Associated Press. *Hiker Rescued from Mt. Washington May Have to Foot the Bill*. 2019. https://www.wmur.com/article/hiker-rescued-from-mt-washington-may-have-to-foot-the-bill/28089803 (accessed August 23, 2023).

Aurelius, Marcus. "The Meditations." *MIT Classics*. 167. http://classics.mit.edu/Antoninus/meditations.8.eight.html (accessed September 5, 2023).

Bandi, Ray. *New England Disciple-Makers Network*. n.d. https://www.disciplemakersnetwork.org/ (accessed August 27, 2023).

Boda, Mark J. and McConville, Gordon J., Eds. *Dictionary of the Old Testament: Prophets*. Downers Grove, IL: IVP Academic, 2012.

Bonhoeffer, Dietrich. *Letters and Papers from Prison*. New York, NY: Touchstone, 1997.

Bruckner, James K. *Healthy Human Life: A Biblical Witness*. Eugene, OR: Cascade, 2012.

Card, Michael. Inexpressible: Hesed and the Mystery of God's Lovingkindness. Downers Grove, IL: InterVarsity Press, 2018.

Carlson, Nathaniel A. "Lament: The Biblical Language of Trauma." *Cultural Encounters* 11, No 1 (January, 2015): 53.

Carmichael, Amy. *Edges of His Ways*. Fort Washington, PA: Christian Literature Crusade, 1955.

Carson, D. A. *The Gospel according to John: The Pillar New Testament Commentary*. Grand Rapids, MI: Inter-Varsity Press; W.B. Eerdmans, 1991.

Clark, Nicholas J. "An Uncomfortable Psalm: A Sermon on Psalm 77." *Faith Community Bible Church*. Loudon, NH, 12 12, 2021.

Duncan, Kathleen B. *My Journey through Grief into Grace.* Wichita Falls, TX: R & K Publishing, 2015.

—. What Bereaved Parents Want You to Know (But May Not Say). Wichita Falls, TX: R & K Publishing, 2015.

—. What Grieving Parents Want You to Know. n.d.

Edmunson, Mika. The Power of Unearned Suffering: The Roots and Implications of Martin Luther King, Jr's Theodicy. Lanham, MD: Lexington, 2017.

Estes, Steve and Tada, Joni Eareckson. "Which God is in Your Sufferings?" *The Journal of Biblical Counseling*, 2004: 21-43.

Faith Community Bible Church. "Elder Vision Priorities." Loudon, New Hampshire, 2018.

Foster, Richard J. Celebration of Discipline: The Path to Spiritual Growth. San Francisco: Harper & Row, 1978.

Francis Chan and Lisa Chan. *You and Me Forever: Marriage in Light of Eternity.* San Fransisco, CA: Claire Love Publishing, 2014.

Guild, Sonny. "The Ministry of Presence: A Biblical View." *Leaven (Pepperdine University), Volume 2, Issue 2*, January 1, 1992.

Harris, Glen E., Jr. "A Wounded Warrior Looks at Psalm 13." *The Journal of Pastoral Theology*, 2010.

Haugk, Kenneth C. Don't Sing Songs to a Heavy Heart: How to Relate to Those Who Are Suffering. St Louis, MO: Stephen Ministries, 2004.

Johnson, Andy. *Missions: How the Local Church Goes Global.* Wheaton, IL: Crossway, 2017.

Matt Boswell and Matt Papa. Our Sins They Are Many, His Mercy is More. 2016.

Moore, Gary. "Samuel: His Call, Service, and Rejection." *Faith Community Bible Church.* Loudon, New Hampshire, January 1, 2023.

Nichols, Andrew and Thorne, Helen. *Real Change: Becoming More Like Jesus in Everyday Life.* Greensboro, NC: New Growth Press, 2018.

Piper, John and Taylor, Justin, eds. *Suffering and the Sovereignty of God.* Wheaton, IL: Crossway, 2006.

Piper, John. "Counseling with Suffering People." *DesiringGod.* February 1, 2003. https://www.desiringgod.org/articles/counseling-with-suffering-people .

Powlison, Daivd. "X-ray Questions: Drawing out the Whys and Wherefores of Human Behavior." *The Journal of Biblical Counseling*, 1999: 2-9.

—. "Familial Counseling: The Paradigm for Familial Counselor-Counselee Relationships in 1 Thessalonians 5." *The Journal of Biblical Counseling*, 2007: 2-16.

—. "The Pastor as Counselor." *The Journal of Biblical Counseling*, 2012: 26-39.

—. The Pastor as Counselor: The Call for Soul Care. Wheaton, IL: Crossway, 2021.

Rojerson, J.W. and McKay, J.W. *The Cambridge Bible Commentary on the New English Bible: Psalms 1-50.* Cambridge: Cambridge University Press, 1977.

Roosevelt, Theodore. "Citizenship in a Republic." *Theodore Roosevelt Association.* 1910. https://theodoreroosevelt.org/ (accessed August 8, 2023).

Shaum, Scott E. The Uninvited Companion: God Shaping Us in His Love through Life's Adversities. Middletown, Delaware: Cresta Riposo, 2017.

Spafford, Horatio Gates. *It Is Well with My Soul.* 1873.

Spurgeon, Charles H. "A Sorrowful Man's Question." *Spurgeon Gems.* Oct 8, 1882. https://www.spurgeongems.org/sermon/chs2666.pdf.

Stingley, Mike. "Disciplined Listening." *The Journal of Biblical Counseling*, 1977: 52-56.

ten Boom, Corrie. *The Hiding Place*. New York: Random House, 1982.

The Anglican Church of North America. *The Book of Common Prayer*. Huntington Beach, CA: Anglican Liturgy Press, 2019.

The Navigators. *History of the Navigators*. n.d. https://www.navigators.org/about/history/.

—. Lessons on Assurance: Five Life-Changing Bible Studies and Memory Verses for New Christians. Colorado Springs, CO: NavPress, 2007.

—. *Topical Memory System*. Colorado Springs: NavPress, 2020.

—. "Wheel Illustration." *The Navigators*. n.d. https://www.navigators.org/resource/the-wheel-illustration/ (accessed August 17, 2023).

Tripp, Paul David. Suffering: Gospel Hope When Life Doesn't Make Sense. Wheaton, IL: Crossway, 2018.

Vine, W, Unger, W.F., and White, W. . *Vine's Complete Expository Dictionary of Old and New Testament Words*. Nashville, TN: Thomas Nelson, 1984.

Vroegop, Mark. Dark Clouds, Deep Mercy: Discovering the Grace of Lament. Wheaton, IL: Crossway, 2019.

Waltke, Bruce K. *The Psalms as Christian Lament*. Grand Rapids, MI: Eerdmans, 2014.

Warren, Tish Harrison. *Prayer in the Night: For Those Who Work or Watch or Weep*. Downers Grove, IL: InterVarsity Press, 2021.

Welch, Edward T. "Exalting Pain? Ignoring Pain? What Do We Do with Suffering?" *The Journal of Biblical Counseling*, 1994: 4-19.

—. Side by Side: Walking with Others in Wisdom and Love. Wheaton, IL: Crossway, 2015.

———. *Caring for One Another: 8 Ways to Cultivate Meaningful Relationships*. Wheaton, IL: Crossway, 2018.

———. "Applied Theology of the Person." *Class Lecture*. Christian Counseling and Education Foundation, 2023. Lecture 3.

Whitman, Lauren. *A Painful Past: Healing and Moving Forward*. Phillipsburg, NJ: P&R Publishing, 2020.

Whitney, Donald S. *Spiritual Disciplines for the Christian Life*. Colorado Springs, CO: NavPress, 1991.

ABOUT THE AUTHOR

Pat Testerman is a pastor at Faith Community Bible Church (fcbcnh.org) in Loudon, New Hampshire. Pat met Martha during college at an InterVarsity Christian Fellowship conference. They married after graduation and spent the next two decades traveling around the world with the military before moving to New England.

Pat holds a master's degree in Christian Ministry from North Park Theological Seminary and a Formation Certificate through the Christian Counseling and Education Foundation (CCEF), with whom he is continuing his training. His eclectic careers between the military and the pastorate included law enforcement and the airlines, and he continues to serve as a part-time officer and chaplain in a local police department, and as a board member for North Country Christian Formation (nccfnh.com).

Pat and Martha are blessed to serve in a congregation where discipleship is practiced as the essential core of the Church's mission. They enjoy working on their family farm, activities with their three adult kids, and the natural beauty God has provided in their area.